Called To Serve My Generation

HOW TO FIND PURPOSE IN A NOISY WORLD

Manny Donkor

First UK and World Paperback edition published by Manny Donkor

Copyright © 2022 by Manny Donkor.

First published 2022

The author's rights are fully asserted. The right of Manny Donkor to be identified as the author of this work has been asserted by him in accordance with the Copyright, Design and Patents Act 1988

All rights reserved. No part of this publication may be reproduced, distributed or transmitted in any form or by any means, including photocopying, recording, or other electronic or mechanical methods, without the prior written permission of the publisher, except in the case of brief quotations embodied in critical reviews and certain other noncommercial uses permitted by copyright law. For permission requests, write to the publisher, addressed "Attention: Permissions Coordinator," at the address below.

Manny Donkor

9, The Clay Farm Centre

Hobson Square, Trumpington

Cambridge CB2 9FN, Cambridgeshire UK

www.ServingMyGeneration.com

hello@servingmygeneration.com for general enquiries and book orders

reviews@servingmygeneration.com for book reviews

Manny@servingmygeneration.com to contact Manny Donkor

Book Layout ©2017 BookDesignTemplates.com

The author's rights are fully asserted. The right of Manny Donkor to be identified as the author of this work has been asserted by him in accordance with the Copyright, Design and Patents Act 1988

Unless otherwise indicated, all scripture noted NIV is taken from the Holy Bible, New International Version 1987 by the Zondervan Corporation. Other scripture quotations are taken from the Holy Bible, New King James Version, 2001 Thomas Nelson Publishers.

Called To Serve My Generation Manny Donkor.

ISBN **978-0-9569185-7-4**

Contents

Chapter One Welcome to the World 1
Chapter Two The Case 9
Chapter 3 Charting the rise of David as King and Servant 19
    Pre-Davidic Era 23
Chapter Four How He Served His Generation 37
Chapter Five Who Am I and What Am I Here For? 47
Chapter Six: What Do I Have to Serve My Generation? 59
Chapter Seven: Who Do I Serve with What I Have? ... 73
Chapter Eight: Where Do I Serve My Generation with What I Have? 79
Chapter Nine: Where do I Serve with What I Have? 93
7 Mountains of Culture 93
Chapter Ten: When Do I Serve with What I Have? 105
Chapter Eleven: Harnessing Resources 109
Chapter Twelve: The Full Picture 119
Chapter Thirteen: Serving Our Generation in the Developing World 125
    Strengths, Weaknesses, Opportunities, and Threats in Africa 128

The Diaspora—Africa's Nehemiah?..............................134

This book is dedicated to my mother, Joana Dei Donkor, the one who nurtured me into a man of purpose.

To my dad, Isaac Donkor, thank you for being there.

To my older siblings, Miriam, Cynthia, Susan and Gerald Donkor, thank you all for your amazing support and encouragement

To Kerry, you are simply an amazing person. Thank you for everything!

To those who believe there is more to life than just merely existing; those who yearn to live a life of significance; this is for you!

To each there comes in their lifetime a special moment when they are figuratively tapped on the shoulder and offered the chance to do a very special thing, unique to them and fitted to their talents. What a tragedy if that moment finds them unprepared or unqualified for that which could have been their finest hour.

–Winston Churchill, former British Prime Minister & Statesman

Chapter One
Welcome to the World

Throughout human history, people who have established their mark on humanity have been those who, one way or another, made an impact on their societies. These people influenced their societies by serving it in one capacity or another. Such people are often celebrated for the actions, inactions, decisions, and selfless sacrifice they made for the welfare and betterment of those societies. They range from warriors who were able to rally their nations in arms against the oppression by a major power to national liberators on whose shoulders a nation stood, having fought to assert their territorial sovereignty and everything in between. Indeed, these heroes and heroines have been immortalized in countless portrayal in history books, the creative arts, and in films and documentaries for posterity.

These are people who served their generation—men and women who added value to people by ensuring that the right environment is created for them to thrive. These were people who recognized the intrinsic value in humanity and therefore worked to ensure that it had the room to flourish without any hindrances. They were not prepared to allow any obstacle to disrupt the growth and development of people and society as a whole.

And in their selfless quest for equality, fairness, and justice, these men and women did not just serve their generation. They also laid a benchmark to assess the success of people in the process. In other words, the success of a person in that community was often measured on the basis of positive impact or any meaningful contribution they make to the well-being of the society. And even though such benchmark was often counterproductive, since one's success cannot be measured by the standards set by people of old, it most often became the yardstick successive generations have used in assessing a person's success or lack thereof.

As you read this book, you may remind yourself of the men and women who are memorialized in your nation's history for their exploits as well as contributions they made in making the society and the nation as a whole what it is today. Others too transcend nations and borders as they have come to be recognized as global icons whose selfless courage touched the hearts and minds of many generations. For such people, they are seen as actors who played their roles on the stage of the world and whose performances helped make the society a better place to live. These people rose up to a challenge society was faced with at a pivotal moment in history and who, as a result, were able to rally the masses to move from a time of incredible difficulties to a period of renewed optimism. And such is the level of reverence they enjoy among their people. They are often ascribed godly characteristics as their achievements were something no ordinary person would have been able to do. Freedom fighters, inventors, political and socio-economic leaders, and entrepreneurs (just to mention a few) will fall into this league of extraordinary men and women.

The twentieth century as well as the first few decades of the twenty-first century are filled with people who will occupy this revered status. Mother Theresa, Nelson Mandela, and Mahatma Gandhi are a few of the heroes and heroines. You may also remember a few of such people from your own country or community

What were they famous for? What impact did they have on the societies they lived in? How relevant are their achievements in today's world? How are they remembered in the communities they lived and served? Your answers are as good as mine!

Contrary to the cult status conferred on them by society, they were usually ordinary men and women who, for want of a better, equal, fair, and peaceful society, rose to the challenge that beset their community. But how did they rise to the challenge? How did they stem the tide? How did they quash the issues that threatened to disturb the rhythm of the life they had known in the culture they lived and represented?

As simplistic as it may sound, these people became revered in their communities by simply serving their generation. In doing so, they found meaning and purpose to their lives. In moments when it mattered the most, they came into their own by selflessly laying down their lives so that the wider community could (and can) exist in peace and harmony. Many were okay with potentially sacrificing their lives for the cause. Indeed, many of them died while serving and fulfilling their purposes. They were not looking for fame or recognition, neither were they looking for their names to be in light—far from it.

As Jesus pointed out during his earthly ministry, it was only in laying one's life down for a greater purpose; that of saving mankind by serving them that they were able to pick it (life) up and not just that but finding a sense of purpose to with which to focus their effort, energy and attention on. In other words, *these people served their generation.*

How did they do it? By laying their lives down, identifying and using their innate abilities to help achieve the goals they had for their societies.

Mentioned earlier in this introductory chapter, Nelson Mandela is a prime example of someone who truly served his generation and beyond, leaving behind a legacy for posterity. Even though he is no longer with us, the world remembers him as the man who stood up to a repressive system of government geared toward oppressing and subjugating a session of society on the basis of skin color. As a lawyer in a predominantly white South Africa under Apartheid, he was consumed with seeing fairness and the equitable distribution of wealth as well as the desegregation and the rule of law established in the country. To these ideals, he committed his life, even to the extent of risking incarceration. As part of his of modus operandi, he was able to use his legal expertise (for he was a fine lawyer!) to fight against the Apartheid system, often earning him a lot of enemies within the country but equally a lot of admirers, sympathy, and friends. For his passion, he was prepared to lay his life down for the underprivileged black majority in the country. And for this, he was incarcerated for twenty-seven years, often refusing to compromise for his own comfort. In doing so, not only was he serving his generation at the time, but he was also looking into the future and for posterity. Mandela found his life's purpose in that prison cell on Robben Island.

As a result of his passion, the country embraced the idea of a free, equal, and fair society with a fully-fledged democracy, which he headed as the first black President of a democratic South Africa. He also became a symbol of integrity, as well as the voice of reason in an increasingly divided, polarized world.

Today, even though he is no longer with us, his legacy still lives on in the hearts of the people for whom he laid down his life. South Africa, the country he fought hard to liberate from the shackles of Apartheid, has been a member of the free democratic world since 1992. And although the rainbow nation still grapples with the residues of its Apartheid, it is in a much better state, post-Mandela. As a result of his legacy, he has also become a global icon for peace, having received many awards for his passion and commitment to world justice and harmony.

Whichever way you look at him, Nelson Mandela, without a shadow of doubt, served his generation with his knowledge of equality and justice, skills as a fine legal brain, as well as and more importantly with his life. This feat has been portrayed variously in films, two of which were *Invictus* and *Mandela*—both biopics.

Mandela and the other examples mentioned earlier, including people in your community, are representations of how ordinary people can rise to the challenge in their world, and by doing so, serve their generation and posterity. These people have also shown that when we serve our generation by heeding its challenges, we find our true identity and purpose for existence.

The quest for significance through serving humanity is what this book is about. This book is a rallying cry to the young and emerging generation, for purpose and meaning to be birthed in them. The primary aim of *Called to Serve My Generation* is to *ignite* a passion among the emerging generation, those who are the future leaders, and who are seeking for a path to a fulfilled and meaningful life. This book is written to inspire a generation toward purposeful living, so that this legacy will be passed on from one generation to the next one.

It is quite ironic that in a world which is increasingly becoming post-modern and knowledge-driven, thanks largely to technology and its resulting opportunities, it is

also a world in which many people still struggle with finding true purpose and meaning in life—signified in the questions they often ask and ponder. Some of the most frequently asked questions among many an emerging generation have been:
- What is God's will for my life?
- What have I been put on this earth to do?
- What is my purpose in life?
- Is there more to life than this life of existence?
- How do I find happiness and fulfillment in life?

Each of these questions points to a deep-seated yearning that every human being has for a sense of identity, purpose, and meaning. They point to the fact that we were born into this world to have a significant impact. We were created with the express desire of adding value or something significant to the world. We were not created to merely exist or survive on the earth. Thus, the questions on the minds of many people, and particularly young people, are a cry for direction: reaching out to identify one's true calling, mission, or purpose in life. They are also the questions that will continue to be asked for generations to come, as people come to terms with their own sense of worth, identity, and purpose.

It is therefore the intention of this book to set you on the journey of discovery as it seeks to guide you, the reader, on the road to discovery. Indeed, this book does not lay claim to all the answers to the issues of life, and neither does it seek to give you specific answers about your true meaning and purpose in life. Certainly, the author is the NOT the creator of life. Like you, he is also on the journey of discovery, and having traveled far enough, has been able to find some of the answers to the big questions about purpose. Through the pages of this book, he hopes to help bring encouragement to you as you also set off on this adventure.

In many ways, this journey is probably one that you will continue until you see corruption. That's because, while you will discover the truth about the purpose and meaning of life, it will not all happen in one go. The answers to your deep yearnings will be given in phases as you navigate your way through life. Patience is required to go through these seasons of frustrations, wanderings, and self-discovery.

In leading you on this journey of discovery, the book will stand on the shoulders of those who have been on this road. It focuses on one historical figure whose journey provides a great example of what happens when we pursue a life of purpose.

The Bible, our primary source of stories of men and women who have been on this journey before, describes such people as *cloud of witnesses* who through perseverance as well as laying aside stumbling blocks (weight of sin) run their race of life successfully (Hebrews 12:1-2). The example of these believers provides us with the roadmap for our journey. We are blessed with the example of one such person—*David, the King of Israel*, about whom a lot has been said and written. Through his story, we hope to receive insight and wisdom to help us navigate our way on the journey of discovery.

Before we delve into the life of our central character—David—I encourage you to keep an open mind and to be attentive to the incredible wealth of wisdom and direction that will be shared within the pages of this book.

It is the hope of the author that by the time you go through the chapters, you will receive momentum for the journey ahead. You will also be provided with indicators to point you in the right direction of finding answers to the questions of purpose.

As the writer of the book, as well as someone who has been on the journey, and who is still on this journey of discovery, I do hope that I would have done my best in leading you on the right path. I do earnestly hope that this book will spark a new fire in you, kick-starting your quest to find your life's purpose. There is nothing more satisfying and fulfilling than knowing that you are in your zone, as originally designed by the creator, architect, and designer of your life—God!

With this in mind, grab yourself a coffee, tea, pen, or pencil and get ready. After all, a journey of a thousand miles begins with the first step. Get ready to take your first step.

Chapter Two
The Case

If you are like me, you enjoy great conversations with people who have made significant contributions to their society. Such people include presidents of nations, grassroots social activists and entrepreneurs who are helping to keep the economic engines of countries running. Such conversations are fascinating to listen to as one learns how the worldview of these people were formed and how such a world view has shaped their character.

One of the questions they are often asked is what they would like to be remembered for. They are asked a question which goes like this: *at the end of your life, how would you like to be remembered?* What would your legacy for society be? The answer to this question reveals a lot about the person.

A thousand years after the death of David, the former king of Ancient Israel, the Apostle Paul reflected on how David was remembered. This is recorded by Luke, a physician and one of the disciples of Jesus Christ in the Acts of the Apostles.

Paul reflects:

> *"Now when David had served God's purpose in his own generation, he fell asleep; he was buried with his ancestors and his body decayed."*

Acts 13:36 (NIV)

The New King James Version of the Bible puts it this way:

> "For David, after he had served his own generation by the will of God, fell asleep, was buried with his fathers, and saw corruption."
>
> Acts 13:36 (NKJV)

This is such an important passage of scripture which summarizes the life of, arguably, the greatest king in the history of ancient Israel. Thus, if David, like those others who have contributed immensely to humanity, was asked how he would like to be remembered, he would perhaps have said: he would like to remembered as the king who served his generation and not according to his own will but rather, by the will of the God who enthroned him as king of Israel. This statement is very important, because within the passage, David's life is contrasted with that of Jesus Christ. It highlights the significance of why it is vitally important to live our lives to the fullest, as eternity cannot be guaranteed, unlike Jesus whom God raised from the dead and therefore did not *see corruption* (v. 37).

The scriptural reference also contains a number of key phrases and words which sum up the life of our subject and which needs a closer look. Thus, for us to set the tone for the thesis of this book, it is imperative that we take a closer look at the following phrases and words:

- *Served*
- *(His) own generation*
- *(By) the will of God*
- *Fell/Fall asleep*
- *Saw/see corruption*

Serve

This is perhaps one of the most important words in the English language, or any other language for that matter, and one that is often difficult if not impossible to live by. According to the scripture, David *served*. What does that mean? What does that mean to us now in the twenty first century, post-Christian, secular culture?

Among other things, to *serve,* evokes the following ideas:
- *To render assistance, to be of use or help*
- *To carry or distribute portions of food and drinks to a patron or specific person or people as a waiter or waitress.*
- *To have a definite use*
- *To perform, do, complete, go through, fulfill, pass, discharge a task (synonym)*

From the definitions above, it is clear that when one serves a person or a group of people, one is rendering assistance or being of help to them. By doing so, you are also having a definite use or what we will describe as purpose. Thus, *a life of purpose is a life of service!*

(Own) Generation

We often use this word to describe a group of people in a society. It also, among other things, describes the characteristic features associated with a group of people. *Generation* can be defined as:
- The entire body of individuals born and living at about the same time
- The term of years roughly thirty years between when they are born and when the next generation is born
- A group of individuals, most of whom are of the same approximate age, having similar ideas, problems, attitudes etc.
- Age group, peer group (synonym)
- Age, period, era, time, etc. (synonyms)

David served by being of definite use to the people of his day: Israelites of the same approximate age who faced threats to their existence as God's chosen people both from within and without. And as we shall look in greater details in the next few chapters, David served his purpose by solving the problems of Israel's right to exist as a sovereign nation under God.

Similarly, in order to serve our generation, it is imperative that we understand the factors that have shaped members of that generation so that we can be able to offer solutions to their challenges. Failure to recognize these factors will lead to us remaining on the margins of society, not being able to effectively bring clarity and the moral leadership needed to tackle problems associated with the popular culture of our day. Perhaps, and significantly, we risk failing that generation simply because we failed to recognize or identify the fundamental issues they face on a daily basis. And in the words of our Lord Jesus Christ, we will fail in becoming the *salt* and *light* of our generation (Matthew 5:13-16). We would lose our ability to preserve as well as bring flavor to our generation. Additionally, we cease to be the torch bearers bringing illumination to light the paths of many an emerging generation.

As a result, it is important we identify the generation we have been called to, so that we can be effective in serving them. If we try to serve everybody in our quest to be solution-carriers, we may not be able to define our point of effectiveness.

Like David, we cannot serve people whom we don't understand or relate to. This is because when God calls us, he calls us to a specific group of people: people who live in a world we are familiar with—a world based on shared experiences, a world where we all grapple with similar challenges as well as the paths we navigate as we embark on our race of life.

Hence, to serve our generation, we must find a need and provide solutions to this need. And we will be at our most effective when we fulfill the purpose of providing contemporary solutions to the issues faced by the generation we are called to serve, since these problems are the issues close to home. They are part of our shared experiences. This is the sure pathway to victorious life.

This book is written with the hope of being of definite use to the current generation; a generation I have referred to as *emerging*. It is purposely written to render assistance in helping the *emerging generation* to also identify their purpose so that they can also be of definite use to their generation and the ones to come. This, they will do by serving them with passion, meaning, and purpose.

Typically, these characteristic features identify members of the *emerging generation*:
- They tend to be global, social, visual, and technological in outlook.
- They are the most connected, educated and sophisticated generation to date.
- They are the teens, the youths, and young adults of our global society.
- They are early adapters, the brand influencers, the social media drivers, the pop culture leaders.
- They don't just represent the future; they are creating or shaping it.
- They are digitally transformed, seamlessly integrating technology into their everyday reality.
- They are sometimes narcissistic, often labelled as self-absorbed, attention-seekers, having an entitlement mentality or mindset.
- They also have a sense of wanting to change the world from what it currently is.
- They are pragmatic when it comes to generating ideas on how to make the world a better place.

- Typically, within the seventeen through thirty-eight-year-old demographic group

Thus, to serve this generation, it is important that we understand the factors that have shaped their lives so that we can be able to offer paths or solutions to their challenges. Hence, the book is written with the emerging generation in mind. It is written to help steer the emerging generation on the journey to find meaning and a sense of purpose to life so that when they have successfully run with perseverance, their race of life, it can be said of them "well done good and faithful servant."

Will of God

There is something unique about pursuing goals and aspirations that are consistent with an arranged purpose. This is what makes the difference between living a life of significance, even if for a short lifetime, and living a life of mediocrity. There is a universal law which recognizes that our human existence has definite purpose and that we are not considered to have lived life to the fullest without us pursuing that purpose. This is the will of God.

Why *Will of God*? This is simply because I believe we all have a definite mandate on our lives when we are born into the world. We often hear people say they weren't living until they found their true life's calling—be it what they choose it to be- and that brought meaning and purpose to their lives. Indeed, throughout the Bible, there are many examples of men and women who sprang to life when they were shown their life's purpose as preordained by God before the foundations of the world. A good example of this is the commissioning of the prophet Jeremiah. This is what was written about him:

> *"The Word of the Lord came to me saying 'Before I formed you in the womb, I knew you, before you were born I set you apart. I appointed you as a prophet to the nations.'"*

Jeremiah 1:4-5 (NIV)

There is a clear indication of the will of God for Jeremiah; that was to be a prophet, God's mouthpiece to the nations, and Israel in particular.

Another example of the will of God for someone is for the Apostle Paul, the man credited with penning about half of the New Testament. In a lot of ways, Paul represents a person who goes totally opposite to the will of God for his life initially, but then comes around to identifying it. Having done that, he spent the rest of his life passionately pursuing his God-ordained purpose. Indeed, he talks about how he went from strongly opposing the very thing he was ordained to defend, right until his 'Damascus' moment, when he makes a full 360-degree turn and, in the process, finds his true purpose for living:

> *"I want you to know, brothers and sisters that the gospel I preached is not of human origin. I did not receive it from any man, nor was I taught it; rather, I received it by revelation from Jesus Christ.*
>
> *For you have heard of my previous way of life in Judaism, how intensely I persecuted the church of God and tried to destroy it. I was advancing in Judaism beyond many of my own age among my people and was extremely zealous for the traditions of my fathers.*
>
> *But when God, who set me apart from my mother's womb and called me by grace, was pleased to reveal his son in me so that I might preach him among the Gentiles, my immediate response was not to consult any human being."*

Galatians 1:11-16 (NIV, emphasis added)

When it became apparent to Paul that God had ordained him to declare the gospel of Jesus's death and resurrection, thus making him the definitive authority and spokesperson for God, there was no need for human affirmation. He jumped right into it, reaching to his target audience—the Gentiles. This is what pursuing the will of God is. And today, we are offered a unique example through

Paul's life, of how important it is to know the will of God and having identified it, to pursue it with passion.

Like Paul the Apostle, David pursued the will of God as a king of Israel, ensuring that the nation of Israel was in a position to continue worshipping God and serving as his model to the world. Thus, it is God who places us where we are so that we can serve our generation.

Fell/Fall Asleep

In the portion of scripture from Acts (13:36), the phrase *fall/fell asleep* is a euphemism which means that David died after he had served his generation by the will of God. It is also a phrase which highlights a very important fact about life—that we do not have eternity to pursue the will of God in our lives. Thus, while we still have today, it is the perfect time to start on that journey. In other words, we do not have eternity to fulfill our divine assignment. Thus, between now and when we die, you and I must do something significant with our lives.

David fulfilled a decree of God in his service to his generation at the time. He did all the service which God, from eternity, had willed that David should do. This is the very heart of this book—to set you on that journey of identifying the will of God and having identified it, pursue it with every fiber of your being and with passion. For in that pursuit lies our purpose and the meaning to our lives.

To this end, there are a couple of observations which hopefully should give us something to ponder on as we go through this journey of identification and the pursuing of our God-ordained mandate:

- To *fall asleep* before we have served our generation is nothing short of tragic.
- It is good to sleep at last, as all our honored fathers and mothers have, but it is a moral calamity

to sleep without having labored to bless the world.
- No man has any right to die until he has put mankind in debt to God through him.
- Every servant of God is immortal until his work is done.
- The grave will be a blessed bed of rest for the man who has served his own generation according to the will of God.
- At the end of your life, how would you like to be remembered?

These thoughts and questions will help set the pace of our journey throughout the book as we find out how we can find the will of God for our lives.

A book of this magnitude will not be complete without a detailed look at the life of the central character - David; the man who served his generation by the will of God. In the next chapters, we will be looking at how David came to serve his generation and how he went about doing it

Chapter 3
Charting the rise of David as King and Servant

In the previous chapter, we learned that David served his generation by the will of God after which *he saw corruption*—a reference to the fact that he died. But how did he serve his generation? And in what capacity did he serve his generation? These are fundamental questions which will help shed light on David's life as an important figure in the history of ancient Israel.

There is no denying the fact that David was considered to be the greatest king to have ruled in the history of Israel, at least if not one of the greatest. His reign became the benchmark for successive kings as he set a precedent for rulership in ancient Israel. Indeed, such was his level of kingship that God promised that there will never, in the nation's history, cease to be a descendant of David on the throne as long as Israel remains as his chosen people (1 Kings 9:5).

It is also worth pointing out that David, with all the pomp and pageantry that accompanied his coronation as well as his divine ordination, was also seen as your average or normal human being. He was subject to like passions, and found himself involved in many personal, family, and national problems. However, these problems did not prevent him from serving his generation, more so by the will of God. Indeed, God in his approval of David, described him as a man after God's own heart (1 Samuel 13:14). This insight will point to God's criteria in choosing a vessel for his work of service. He qualifies those he chooses and even though a person might have a character or moral flaw, God still uses them because he is the only one who could qualify his *called-out* ones for the assignment he has for them.

Again, it is worth pointing out that the reasons why God chose David, a man after his own heart, despite his moral lapses, are the following:

David was humble—He was humble enough to acknowledge his flaws and failings and went before God in repentance. Psalm 51 is the perfect expression of remorse and a repentant heart. As he rightly pointed out, God would not and did not reject (Psalm 51:17). "Lowborn men are but a breath, the highborn are but a lie; if weighed on a balance, they are nothing; together they are only a breath" (Psalm 62:9 NIV).

- *David was reverent*—David, during his reign as king in Israel, showed a deep and solemn respect for God and his creation. Thus, on several occasions, when he had the perfect opportunity to eliminate the one person standing in his way to kingship, he decided against it; as Saul was still the Lord's ordained king at the time. On both occasions, he reiterated the fact that he had no right to eliminate a king who was ordained by God. *"I called to the Lord, who is worthy of praise, and I have been saved from my enemies"* (Psalm 18:3 NIV).
- *David was respectful*—Again, such was the level of respect he had for God and his will, that he

was not willing to compromise on taking steps without God's leading. We also know that in spite of these, he also had *hubris*.
- *David was repentant*—For all his moral flaws and failings, there was one thing that separated him from all kings in Israel: that he was humble enough to recognize his failing and, most importantly, be repentant by asking God for forgiveness. Again, Psalm 51 reminds us of this.
- *David was obedient*—It is no surprise that David was a man after God's own heart, as on many occasions, he was obedient to divine instructions. He enquired of the Lord whether it was the right time to pursue his enemies and only proceeded when he was given the all-clear by God. In a nutshell, he did whatever God wanted him to do.
- *David had absolute faith in God*—To say that David couldn't have been a man after God's own heart would be a gross understatement of the man, especially considering the fact that there was no man in the known world at the time who had absolute faith and thus was utterly devoted to God more than David was. He demonstrated this in his encounter with Goliath, the champion from Gath. Shortly before the duel, we saw direct evidence of David's faith when he said:

"The Lord who delivered me from the paw of the lion and from the paw of the bear will deliver me from the hand of the Philistine..." (1 Samuel 17:37 ESV)

David was fully aware that God was in control of his life and he had faith that God would deliver him from impending danger.

- *David absolutely loved God's law*—Of the 150 Psalms in the Bible, David is credited with penning over half of them. Writing at various and often troubling times in his life, David repeatedly mentioned how much he loved God's perfect word. A good example of this is found in Psalm 119:47-48:

"For I delight in your commands because I love them. I lift up my hands to your commands, which I love and I meditate on your decrees."

So how did David serve his generation by the will of God? He served his generation in three ways:
- *As a shepherd boy*
- *As an army general*
- *As a king*

And he distinguished himself in all three areas —the subject of much of this chapter and the next one.

However, in order for us to delve deep into the life of David and how he served his generation in all three spheres, it is important that we look at the historical and political contexts leading up to his ascent to the throne. Doing a due diligence of this part of his story would give us a sense of appreciation of the conditions existing at the time prior to his enthronement and what happened after that. Thus, we will be able to see why David was chosen as the ideal ruler in Israel. More importantly, we will see why David served his generation as well as the reasons why God placed his confidence in his ability to carry out his divine assignment as a shepherd boy, an army general, and a king.

Pre-Davidic Era

Before David became king in ancient Israel, the nation had a special relationship with God as their Protector going back to the time of the patriarch Abraham. When Israel became a nation made up of 12 tribes, their very existence as a nation depended solely on their relationship with God. And to further cement this relationship, there was a structure of governance; call it an administrative structure by which the new nation lived and functioned. This was called *Theocracy*.

At best, the system of governance could be described as a *commonwealth of Israel*, covering the time of Moses right up to the coronation of Saul as king in Israel.

Derived from two Greek words—*Theo* meaning god and *krateos* meaning to rule—it represents a government structure in which God or a deity is the supreme leader over the people. A working definition of *Theocracy* is that it is a form of government in which a deity of some type is recognized as the supreme-being ruling authority, giving divine guidance to human intermediaries that manage the day-to-day affairs of the government. This is the best description of the government structure in ancient Israel at the time. The Israelites were a special people to God and he, in turn, was their supreme leader in the strong sense of the word. He, however, governed them through intermediaries who were his mouthpiece, delivering instructions on how to live as a nation. He also took on the sole responsibility of *Defender* of the people, often protecting ancient Israel from neighboring nations which threatened its right to exist as a sovereign nation. Thus, Theocracy was the administration style set up to help govern ancient Israel.

Throughout the Bible, particularly in the Old Testament, we see this government structure rolled out on numerous occasions.

To begin with, the establishment of the nation of Israel kicked off the system in motion. This event is seen during Israel's captivity in Egypt, in which the Israelites were brutally oppressed by a Pharaoh *who did not know Joseph* (Exodus 1:8). And in response to the cry of his people for deliverance, God appointed Moses, who had been raised in the Egyptian royal courts, to speak to Pharaoh to let his people go. Following this instance were the ten plagues which wreaked havoc on the Egyptian nation and demonstrated God's power over the earth but more importantly proved God as the ultimate Defender of his people. This led to their eventual release from slavery at the hands of the Egyptians.

After their exodus from Egypt, God, through his mouthpieces, established laws, rules, and regulations by which the people were to live: laws and regulations that heavily underpin our modern way of life today. Under theocracy, we saw the relationship between God and his people flourish even with all the rejection and the betrayal of loyalty that ancient Israel showed towards Him. He proved to them on various occasions that his word was his bond. On those occasions, God came to their aid, helping them defeat their enemies and reestablishing peace and a new devotion to Him. This, he did mainly through men and women from among them who were empowered and rose up to lead the people into battle with their enemies, with the Philistines being their arch-nemesis. These hero-liberators became known as Judges. The likes of Gideon, Deborah, Samson, Barak, and Jephthah are a few of these ordinary men and women who were called and qualified by God to help liberate his people from the hands of their enemies.

However, this government system was tested on various occasions as the people continued to flirt with heathen gods and a secular lifestyle. Such was the level of rejection of Theocracy that by the time of Samuel and his children, this momentum had reached a climax leading to the open and popular demand for the scrapping of the old system in favor of a monarchy. The push for monarchy was exacerbated by a failure in leadership during Samuel's stewardship in Israel.

Fed up with the corrupt practices and leadership of Samuel's children, the people made a representation to Samuel, who was frail and old at the time, demanding the institution of monarchy as the preferred system of government in Israel. This is how the account is presented in the Bible:

> "When Samuel grew old, he appointed his sons as Israel's leaders. The name of his first born was Joel and the name of his second was Abijah, and they served at Beersheba. But his sons did not follow his ways. They turned aside after dishonest gains and accepted bribes and perverted justice.
>
> So all the elders of Israel gathered together and came to Samuel at Ramah. They said to him: 'you are old, and your sons do not follow your ways; now appoint a king to lead us such as all the other nations have ... we want a king over us. Then we will be like all the other nations, with a king to lead us and to go out before us and fight our battles.'"

1 Samuel 8:1-4, 19 (NIV)

Even though Samuel tried to persuade them to drop their demand, warning them of the consequences of instituting a monarchy in which the king will virtually treat them like slaves—a sharp reminder of their four hundred years of slavery in Egypt — even that was not enough to deter them from their demands. And although the reasons that gave rise to the demand—that of the corrupt leadership of Abijah and Joel—their main reason was rather shallow and cosmetic.

Having looked around and observed how their neighboring nations had rulers who were also military men and who led their people to war, they saw that as being the standard. They felt they fell far short of this example under a theocratic structure of governance, with God as the leader and ultimate defender. The Israelites had a fantasy of having a king, who as the commander-in-chief, would lead them into battle against their enemy. The truth, however, was that they were not like all the other nations. They were a special people consecrated to God. He was their God, Leader, Deliverer, and ultimate Defender and they were his people consecrated wholly to him. But they had other ideas.

Their demand for a king was a clear rejection of God and his governing structure under theocracy. He prepared them for the granting of their wish as this led to the search, preparation, and the crowning of Saul, the son of Kish, as the first monarch in Israel. However, the pomp, pageantry, and euphoria that greeted Saul's coronation soon gave way to disappointment as lack of leadership, failure to live up to expectations, disobedience (which in turn threw Israel into a period of upheaval), uncertainty, and lack of clarity and direction for the new administration, characterized his time as first king of Israel. This set of circumstances will later lead to dire consequences for ancient Israel, the worst of which was the splitting of the nation into two factions. There was the Northern Kingdom, which comprised of first eleven tribes with Shechem as their capital, and the Southern Kingdom which was comprised of Judah with Hebron as the capital.

Two events gave rise to the lack of leadership and woeful disobedience of commands by Saul.

The first event of the departure is recorded in 1 Samuel 13. In one of several encounters with the Philistines, Saul was instructed by Samuel to wait for the priestly ritual to be performed before he could lead the Israelite army into battle. With the time fast approaching for the battle lines to be drawn and yet no sign of Samuel, he usurped the priestly function when he said *"Bring me the burnt offering and the fellowship offering"* (1 Samuel 13:9). Once he had gone ahead and performed the ritual in direct contravention of the law, Samuel appeared to denounce Saul's flouting of God's instruction, and with it, his rejection as the king of Israel. This is what Samuel said in his rebuke of Saul:

> *"'You have done a foolish thing' Samuel said. 'You have not kept the command the Lord your God gave you; if you had, he would have established your kingdom over Israel for all time. But now your kingdom will not endure; the Lord has sought out a man after his own heart and appointed him ruler over his people, because you have not kept the Lord's command.'"*

1 Samuel 13:13-14 (NIV)

Thus, this pronouncement spelled the beginning of the end for Israel's first king.

The second event which exacerbated Saul's leadership problems is recorded in 1 Samuel 15. In this account, Saul is again instructed to totally destroy the Amalekites for

"...what they did to Israel. When they waylaid them as they came up from Egypt. Now go, attack the Amalekites and totally destroy all that belongs to them. Do not spare them; put to death men and women, children and infants, cattle and sheep, camels and donkeys."

1 Samuel 15:2-3 (NIV)

On this occasion too, Saul disobeys God's instruction by saving the best of the spoils of the military campaign, sparing Agag, the Amalekite king, alongside the booty from the war. God expressed his disappointment at Saul's disobedience when he told Samuel that *"I regret that I have made Saul king, because he has turned away from me and has not carried out my instructions..."* (1 Samuel 15:11 NIV).

On this occasion, as it transpired in the battle at Michmash, Saul is rebuked for not following through with instructions. This is what Samuel said:

> "...'Although you were once small in your own eyes, did you not become the head of the tribes of Israel? The Lord anointed you as king over Israel. And he sent you on a mission, saying, 'Go and completely destroy those wicked people, the Amalekites; wage war against them until you have wiped them out.' Why did you not obey the Lord? Why did you pounce on the plunder and do evil in the eyes of the Lord?'"

1 Samuel 15:17-19 (NIV)

In his last words to Saul, Samuel made these strong remarks about what was to become of him:

> "'Does the Lord delight in burnt offerings and sacrifices as much as in obeying the Lord? To obey is better than sacrifice, and to heed is better than the fat of rams. For rebellion is like the sin of divination and arrogance like the evil of idolatry. Because you have rejected the word of the Lord, he has rejected you as king."

1Samuel 15:22-23 (NIV)

From both accounts, we see a king on whose shoulders so much was expected in this new era of monarchy in Israel, fall from grace because of his flaw—a blatant disregard for God's instructions. This fall was two-dimensional—spiritual and physical.

Spiritually, the covering and protection which had come upon him in the lead up to his crowning as king of Israel and subsequent reign left him only to be replaced by an evil spirit which tormented him. He was never the same afterwards.

Physically, he became depressed, often needing David to skillfully play the harp to soothe his malady. He also became erratic in his judgment and this clouded his fitness to rule as Israel's king. He became paranoid in the process, pursuing people he saw as threat to his kingship, and potentially establishing a dynasty with Jonathan, his son, as the next heir to the throne. This perceived threat led him on a campaign to eliminate the threats to the throne, in particular David, who by now had been secretly anointed as his successor and was patiently waiting in the wings.

As a result, he left Israel in an unstable, shaky, and uncertain state as he could no longer rule with confidence and the authority the office of the king quite rightly demanded. In the end, Saul died a lonely figure, having previously tried to fortify his kingship by seeking the help of the witch of Endor. He died by throwing himself on a spear during a battle with Israel's arch enemy, the Philistines.

It was during this vulnerable, weakened, and uncertain time in Israel's history that David rose to reestablish the kingship and the sovereignty of Israel as a strong united nation under God.

The Davidic Era

Out with the old! In comes the new! This is what precedes the ushering in of a new era in any endeavor and one would expect that this is what happened with David's ascent to the throne as the second king of Israel. However, this is far from what actually happened. In fact, it would take many years after his anointing and public announcement before David would eventually become king. Nonetheless, his reign, which lasted for forty years, heralded a golden age in the history of Israel, as the nation of God's people enjoyed relative peace and stability and with it the much-needed socio-economic development in the nation.

The circumstances leading to David's rise to the throne is a sharp reminder of what happens when we fail to execute a divine agenda. Through the experience, we learn that God always has a backup plan when the original one does not go according to schedule. We can also see how God chooses, qualifies, and calls people with the right heart and attitude, whom he commissions to get the job done.

In 1 Samuel 16, God instructs Samuel to choose Saul's successor from the house of Jesse the Bethlehemite, after rejecting Saul as king (1 Samuel 16:1). This choice was to take place while Saul was still the de-facto king of Israel. Hence, the selection and anointing ceremony had to be done in secret, for fear that Saul might be enraged and seek to stop the ceremony from going ahead.

In the selection process, Samuel is guided by his senses and so perceives that the first son of Jesse, Eliab was physically primed king material. But unlike Samuel, God as the king-maker had other plans. He points this out to Samuel:

> *"...Do not consider his (Eliab) appearance or his height, for I have rejected him. The Lord does look at the things people look at. People look at the outward appearance, but the Lord looks at the heart."*
>
> 1Samuel 16:7 (NIV)

We are reminded once again through this encounter that God always chooses people that have the needed skills and abilities, even if these are not evident. This reminder should reassure many an emerging generation who might have issues with whether they have what it takes to serve their generation. God always qualifies the ones he calls and prepares them for the task ahead.

After a frantic search without success, a lot falls firmly on the lap of David, the last of Jesse's children. He is the least qualified in people's eyes, but clearly the one with the heart for leadership. The urgency with which he was brought from tending his father's livestock in the wilderness attests not only to his importance in God's eyes, but also the one who is going to lead Israel into the next season. *"Send for him; we will not sit down until he arrives"* (1 Samuel 16:11 NIV).

And with this prompt enters David, the teenage shepherd boy who had been manning his father's livestock in the wilderness. The relatively unknown, untested, shepherd boy is the person Samuel is instructed to *"arise and anoint him, this is the one"* (1 Samuel 16:12b). He is then anointed in his shepherd clothes, possibly covered in dust, mud, and with a shepherd's staff in his hand. He is God's chosen vessel who would eventually take over from Saul.

In his first appearance as a teenage shepherd boy, David is described as *"glowing with health"* as well as having *"a fine appearance and handsome features."* Some versions of the Bible described him as having *"a ruddy complexion"* (having a healthy red color of the skin) with *"beautiful eyes"* and *"a handsome appearance"* (AMP). The King James Bible also describes young David as being *"ruddy"* and *"withal of a beautiful countenance"* and *"goodly to look to."* Clearly, though a teenager, David was a strong, healthy, and handsome young man who could turn a few ladies' heads!

However, David's route to the throne was not straightforward as one would expect, especially when he had a divine mandate to rule as king. Rather, immediately as he was anointed, he went straight back to the wilderness to tend his father's livestock—a far cry from the royal palace that had been much anticipated. For the next few years, he would have to wait for God's green light, especially when a weakened Saul was still the legitimate monarch at the time. As the new sheriff in town, he could have personally or with other co-conspirators engineered his ascent to the throne, since he had been given the divine seal by the ultimate king maker—God. Nonetheless, that was not what happened.

From the time of his anointing and investiture, he would continue in his old job of a shepherd, tending the family livestock trade, often fighting to defend the flock from other ferocious animals like lions and bears. He would also be brought to the royal palace to serve the king, the one he would eventually succeed. And while he was there, he must have witnessed first-hand the business of administering a nation of twelve tribes and other clans. He would have also seen first-hand, the challenges of leadership, along with the many difficult decisions that had to be made. At the royal palace, his purpose was medicinal or healing. He had been recommended and hired to soothe the bouts of depression Saul suffered from. This depression came to Saul as a result of being stripped of his crown due to his lapse in judgment and disobedience.

As in the wilderness with the family livestock, he had to defend himself from the king who clearly saw him as a threat to establishing his kingship, and potentially setting up a dynasty with his son Jonathan as the heir to the throne. On numerous occasions, while discharging his duties, the current but weakened king tried to kill the king-in-waiting. This sub-plot is interesting for all the right reasons.

To begin with, David would have been incensed by these incidents and would have used them as a catalyst in forcing his own ascent to the throne. In fact, in his departure from Saul, David had several opportunities to end the saga by killing Saul when he is edged on by his followers. However, he did not want to touch the *Lord's anointed*—a recognition of the fact that God was still in the business of crowning kings as well as renouncing the ones that had fallen out of favor. As part of his season of waiting, David would chalk an important milestone—a milestone that would eventually cement his kingship and leadership qualities.

In one of the many battles with the Philistines, David, the shepherd boy, comes face to face with Goliath, the giant who had been a fighter and warrior from birth. David, with his experience and skills gained from protecting sheep and goats from lions and bears, spectacularly defeats Goliath with just a sling and a stone. Prior to the battle, David had stuck his claim to the throne by rallying the Israelite army to prepare for a mighty rout. First, this is what he told Saul, and his army generals:

> "David said to Saul, 'let no one lose heart on account of this Philistine; your servant will go and fight him... your servant has been keeping his father's sheep. When a lion or a bear came and carried off a sheep from the flock, I went after it, struck it and... I seized it by its hair, struck it and killed it. Your servant has killed both the lion and the bear; this uncircumcised Philistine will be like one of them, because he had defied the armies of the living God. The Lord who rescued me from the paw of the lion and the paw of the bear will rescue me from the hand of this Philistine.'"
>
> 1Samuel 17:32, 34-37 (NIV)
>
> David, by making this profound statement, was saying that he had a precedent to fall on; it was relevant experience even though he did not look like a warrior material. Physically, he was not of the same stature as Goliath, and this made him curse David, saying, "'Am I a dog that you come at me with sticks? ...Come here,' he said, 'and I'll give your flesh to the birds and the wild animals'" (1 Samuel 17:43 44 NIV). With this, Goliath "cursed David by his gods."

Far from being a novice who could easily be squashed, David was a formidable opponent in a simple teenager's body. His time spent in the wilderness looking after his father's livestock provided him with ample training for the duel. In effect, those moments when he encountered the lions and bears were the moments that helped forge his military prowess and strength. This placed him as the perfect candidate for the battle, considering the fact that the entire hierarchy of the Israelite army, including the commander-in-chief, Saul, was shaking with fear at the sight of the giant Goliath.

We know the end of the story—with just a sling and a stone, David defeated Goliath, and with him a significant victory over their arch enemy for the first time. It is worth pointing out that his victory, far from it being a personal achievement, inspired confidence in the Israelite army who had all but given up on the idea of victory in the battle. David's triumphs over Goliath emboldened the army of Israel to complete the rout by chasing the Philistines down until they were annihilated. And with the victory, came the ushering in of a period of relative peace from external aggressors.

This, however, did not stop Saul from his continued campaign to get rid of David as a direct threat to his authority. If anything at all, Saul turned on the heat as David was beginning to gain popularity among the people. In the end, David went into a self-imposed exile along with a few renegade men who saw something in him, and they often slept alongside with the enemy. All these milestones were the preparations he had to undergo for his reign in Israel.

By the time he was ready, he would also preside over a deeply divided Israel with 11 tribes forming the Northern kingdom with its capital in Shechem, and the tribe of Judah as the Southern kingdom with its capital in Samaria. Having started his reign in the southern kingdom, ruling seven and a half years, he eventually succeeded in uniting both kingdoms into one nation, ruling in the northern kingdom for thirty-three years—making his kingship in united Israel as forty years.

From being anointed as the king-in-waiting, to running for his dear life because he was seen as a threat to the current king, to standing in front of the giant Goliath ready to fight him with nothing more than a sling and a stone, David showed us an example of what it meant to have a promise made about you, and to yet wait in the trenches for a long time before eventually rising to occupy your rightful place.

Even though the journey to the throne was quite excruciating to watch—something that would have easily broken the spirits of many an emerging generation—it served to prepare David for service. Each step of the journey was a learning experience for him, something that would eventually set him up for success as one of the greatest kings if not the greatest king to have ruled in ancient Israel.

We cannot, however, complete a profile of David without highlighting some of the not-so-pleasant elements of his reign. He had moral flaws which eventually blew up into full scale family upheavals, which threatened to derail his kingship. And yet, with all the flaws and inconsistencies, God was still able to put his stamp of approval on him, calling him *"a man after my own heart."* God also fulfilled a promise he made to David when he said that he would establish his dynasty forever. Solomon would rise to succeed but perhaps and more significantly, the messiah Jesus Christ would trace his ancestry to the house of Jesse, the Bethlehemite.

David's story is a timely reminder that God chooses those that he qualifies to do his bidding. Even though they may not have or possess the physical qualities, the one who calls them knows them well and that is all that matters.

We can see that David, as the king of Israel, served his generation in various ways which prompted the apostle Paul to make reference to him. Paul named him as someone who made an impact on the lives of his ancestors—something worth mentioning as an encouragement to people of our need to also follow suit.

David served his generation by the will of God, after which he saw corruption. The questions are, how did he serve his generation, and are there lessons we can draw from his life that can help us navigate our way through the journey of life?

MANNY DONKOR

Chapter Four
How He Served His Generation

There is no denying the fact that David served his generation at the time and that he served with all his abilities. One can therefore see among other things the reason why he was described as a man after God's heart. But how did he serve his generation? And in what capacity did he serve his generation?

From the accounts in the Bible, it seems to suggests that David served his generation by the will of God in three ways—first as a *shepherd*, an *army general* and then as *a king*. An exploration of these capacities will be appropriate as it gives us a sense of the levels in which David functioned in those roles. Each role was intertwined in providing the leadership characteristics which helped shape his reign in Israel. Using this format also provides us with an insight into how he served in those roles.

As a Shepherd

In the Bible, we are first presented with David as the teenager who is in the wilderness caring for his father's livestock. It is this role that provides him with the skills to face and prevail over Goliath who had been a warrior his entire life. So what is it about taking care of sheep and goats that makes David so skillful in the art of war, eventually landing in the palaces of Israel?

One thing is certain and worth pointing out: that God called David from shepherding livestock to shepherding a different flock—his people Israel (2 Samuel 5:2; 2 Samuel 7:7-8; Psalm 78:70-71).

Shepherding is one of the oldest occupations. It is therefore not a surprise that a shepherd's care and relationship with his flock was a common metaphor in the ancient near East for the leadership of people, especially for kingship. Also, various gods of the nations which surrounded Israel were occasionally spoken of as shepherds. Indeed, in the Bible, civic and religious leaders were shepherds, and the imagery is connected to kingship (Psalm 23:1; 1 Kings 22:17).

Trying to imagine David's life as a shepherd is not easy for most urban city dwellers, as we don't often see people herding flocks around our manicured neighborhoods and cities. But shepherding in the ancient world was in many ways simpler than our busy lives; it involved a lot of watching animals as they grazed. But it was far from mundane. To this day, caring for animals always presents unique difficulties, especially with challenges of the environment. We could summarize the life of a shepherd as one of constant caregiving. For instance, David needed to provide food and water for his sheep—not an easy task for a shepherd boy from Bethlehem.

The Bible describes Canaan as a good land, a land of blessing for God's people, but it was not overly lush. Therefore shepherds roamed the hills and valleys far more remote and often rugged regions with marginal rainfall to provide the needed pasture for their flocks. Thus, to provide for his flock, David needed to be a good guide, since the life of a shepherd involved a lot of walking. Each day, he would bring his flock from the safety of the village and wander through the hills and valleys in order to provide enough grass for them to eat. During this daily routine, a shepherd would need to be aware of the needs of his flock as a whole, and the needs of each sheep individually. David therefore knew each one of his sheep and did not let any go astray. He always led them to the best pastures.

Though he was but little thought of, no one could say that David did not do his work well. In fact, there was not a more careful or watchful shepherd on all the hills around Bethlehem. He knew each of his sheep and never allowed them to go astray. He always led them to the best pastures and found the coolest and freshest water for them to drink.

David was also as brave as a lion, and if any wild beast came lurking around hoping to snatch a lamb away, he was up at once and would attack the fiercest beast single-handed. Nothing could ever do harm to his flock. While looking after sheep was the job of the youngest son, this did not deter David from it. Rather, what he learned as a shepherd helped him throughout his life. Among other things, it taught him to look after himself in the wild.

Above all else, his experience as a shepherd taught him about God. Consequently, while others saw a simple shepherd, God saw a king who would serve his people.

In fact, David's life as a shepherd continued to play a role after he left the pasture. Much of what he learned leading sheep, he applied as a leader of people. Famously, he appealed to his exploits in guarding the flock; how he depended on God to illustrate his ability to fight Goliath (1 Samuel 17:34-37). Also, David's experiences as a shepherd found their way into his poetry, providing rich imagery for many of his beloved Psalms, including Psalm 23!

David's life as a shepherd provides a stark reminder of how the most mundane of task can serve as the basis for growth and the development of character traits that can stand us in good stead, both in the present and future. It is therefore imperative that as an emerging generation, we learn vital life lessons from the environment we find ourselves in—whether that be in the home, on the job, school, or even in our social group interactions. These platforms provide the processes needed to engender growth, as well as the formation of grit and determination—all hallmarks for a purposeful and successful life.

As an Army Commander / Warrior

David's role as an army commander and warrior is a significant one. It helped cement his authority as an important leader in Israel at the time, more specifically as the one who helped solidify Israel's position as an important nation.

Militarily, David had already distinguished himself as a strategist and combat-ready prior to his ascent to the throne. When we are introduced to him in first and second Samuel, he is portrayed as a very successful soldier who had chalked a number of victories in many battles. These had not gone unnoticed by the Israelite population, often landing him in trouble with the authorities; Saul to be precise. By the time he became the king of Israel, he had already developed a cadre of well-trained troops. These dedicated and loyal men stood by him when he was fleeing from Saul. These devoted soldiers were ready to follow him anywhere and in fact, they did follow him from the wilderness of Judah through to Gath, Ziklag, Hebron, and finally Jerusalem. These troops later became his personal guard and the core of his regular army.

With the core of his military in place, as well as silencing the common enemy in the Philistines, David was free to expand his kingdom to the east. There, he defeated the Moabites who then became a vassal state, paying tribute to the royal coffers (2 Samuel 8:12). He also fought the Ammonites and defeated them.

Through the expansion, David was able to gain control over international trade routes, which made Israel an important economic power. David became rich from the spoils of war, and tributes were brought to Jerusalem. Even the Phoenician king of Tyre, Hiram, started trading with him especially after he made Jerusalem his capital. Thus, the spoils of war, the levies from administered territories, and the tributes from vassal states all flowed into the royal treasury.

As a King

Undoubtedly the greatest king in the history of Israel, David's reign was characterized by a period of rapid growth and development which established the nation of Israel as a powerful economic and political power in the known world.

For a start, David ensured that the right of Israel to remain a sovereign and peaceful nation was achieved. This he did by engaging in a series of battles with Israel's arch enemy, the Philistines, finally prevailing over them to secure the peace of the nation. Boosted by a well-trained professional army, Israel, under King David, embarked on a territorial expansion program. Through these efforts, the nation expanded its boundaries by conquering and subduing other neighboring nations. The vassal states became a rich source of revenue for the treasury, which then provided the king with the financial backing towards an extensive socio-economic spending program aimed toward Israel's revitalization. Chief among the successes in his military expedition was the capture of the city of Jerusalem and making it the new capital of a united kingdom of Judah and Israel.

The capture of Jerusalem was strategic in providing a neutral place for both kingdoms to call their capital. This helped in unifying the two kingdoms after decades of in-fighting among and between themselves. It was only when David became king that steps were taken to unify both kingdoms.

As a passionate and devoted Yahwist, David took steps to make Jerusalem not only the political capital of a united Israel but also as a very important religious and sacred place for the unbridled worship of the God of Abraham, Isaac and Jacob—his ancestors. Part of the measures to ensure this was bringing the Ark of the Covenant, a symbol of the presence of God among his people, into Jerusalem and giving it a permanent home.

Furthermore, as part of his program of socio-economic development and good neighborliness, he extended a hand of friendship to royals from neighboring nations in a series of agreements for mutual exchange of resources and ideas. A good example is the agreement with King Hiram of Tyre, which, among other things, provided the raw materials needed for David's ambitious infrastructural projects.

As a de-facto king, David established a structured system of administering the new united Israel. He established a professional army with the core being the men who stood by him during his exile from Israel and his predecessor Saul. He also set up a judicial system with elders of the various tribes serving as judges over their people. He often had the final judgment on cases referred to him by the elders. He also had a team of ministers who helped in governing effectively. Among members of his cabinet were Jehoshaphat as recorder (public relations official); Joab as defense secretary or chairman of the Joint Chiefs of Staff; Zadok, Ahimelek, and Abiathar as clergy; and Seraiah as secretary among others (2 Samuel 8:15-15). Together, they helped David in his administration of the affairs of Israel, efficiently and effectively.

As a Yahwist

With Jerusalem becoming the religious center of all of Israel, and with the arrival of the Ark of the Covenant to cement this, the worship of Yahweh became the unifying factor strengthening the bond between Judah and Israel.

From the beginning of his career, David showed himself to be a fervent Yahwist. His religious devotion was confirmed by the presence in his retinue of the priest Abiathar and the prophets of God. David's devotion to Yahweh probably made it easier for the leaders of Israel to accept him as king. He had a deep, unending love for God. He was renowned for his passion for God, his Psalms and musical abilities, his inspiring courage, and his expertise in warfare.

One cannot talk extensively about the life of David without mentioning his devotion to God. Indeed, among his numerous achievements in defeating Goliath, establishing Israel as an economic and political powerhouse at the time, he is also considered as a man who had intense passion and devotion for God. This passion was in spite of his flaws, of which there were many. And he took the necessary steps to ensure that the worship of God was embedded in the national consciousness in Israel.

David established the worship of God in a single place. This is very significant, because up until this point, God had been worshipped wherever the Ark of the Covenant was. It moved around wherever the leaders of the people were based, so it was discovered in different places in Israel. He placed the Ark of the Covenant in a simple place in the capital, and the people went there to worship God. David's choice of Jerusalem as the capital was very successful because the people came to worship God in one central place. And in doing this, David gave the twelve tribes a focus they are able to look to.

Thus, David was effective as a shepherd, an army commander, and a king. The experiences he went through as a youth provided him with the necessary abilities and skills to function effectively in those roles. This ensured that he left a great legacy for posterity. Today, David is remembered as the young shepherd who rose to become a great warrior, a decorated army commander, and a very successful king. And all of these were possible because God saw what others did not see—for others saw a shepherd boy but God saw a king, a man after his own heart. Judging from David's time on earth, one can safely say that God was not disappointed in him.

However, this does not negate his moral failing. In the previous chapter, we noted how his flaws began to unravel, especially during the latter part of his reign. The issue with Bathsheba and the internal insurrection that took place with Absalom are but a few of the problems that plagued his monarchy. However, in spite of this weakness, he was still able to find within himself the humility to admit and confess his shortcomings. This humility is probably the reason why he was still largely successful as a king (Psalm 51).

David's life journey into becoming the man that he was raises fundamental questions for us as an emerging generation, especially as we strive to find purpose and relevance in our lives. Answers to the following questions may invariably provide the blueprint for our journeys as we embark on them.

We will see through this book, but more so in the Bible, how David transformed not only himself but also an entire nation of God's people. As people in a post-modern, post-Christian culture, the dilemma we face is often one of identifying our purpose. Also, how, if we are anything like David, we can also serve our generation as our way of living purposeful lives?

In order to do this, we need to find answers to these simple but fundamental questions:
- What am I here on this earth for?
- What skills/talents do I have to serve my generation?
- Whom should I serve with what I have?
- How do I serve my generation with what I have?
- Where do I serve my generation with what I have?
- When should I serve my generation with what I have?

It is the intention of this book and its author to explore the answers to these fundamental questions in great detail. Doing this will open the door to a life of purpose and fulfillment in many an emerging generation. I therefore entreat you to go on this journey together and as we explore, perhaps, we can come out of this process with a sense of how we can be relevant to our generation—through serving one another.

Chapter Five
Who Am I and What Am I Here For?

We have seen from the previous chapter how David served his generation—as a shepherd, an army general, warrior, and a king. His story draws our attention to the fundamental question often asked: if one is ever going to find purpose in their life. David found his purpose when he served his people—and through his reign, he was able to find his *"for this reason I was born"* moment; something we all go through at some point in our lives, some sooner than others.

In our quest for purpose in life, the first important question to be asked is *"who am I?"* and fundamentally, *"what am I here on earth for?"* These questions are so vital to us identifying our purpose as everything else hinges on it. When we are able to know who we truly are and hence our reason for existence, it provides the grounds from which we are able to identify the *what, why, who* and *how* of serving our generation. This is where identity is realized and solidified. In a time when the subject of identity is being discussed in various circles as well as being redefined, one needs to seek clarity concerning this topic.

A quick look through a dictionary provides different definitions and variations of the definition of identity. Here are a few of them from the Collins English Dictionary:

- The state of having unique identifying characteristics
- The individual characteristics by which a person or thing is recognized for

From Cambridge Dictionary Online:
- Who a person is or the qualities of a person or a group that makes them different from others.
- The reputation, characteristics etc. of a person or organization that makes the public think about them in a particular way.
- Who a person is, or information that proves who a person is; for example, their name and date of birth.

From Merriam-Webster Dictionary Online:
- The distinguishing character or personality of an individual

From the various definitions, there is a common thread that runs through them. Among other things, identity is about:
- An individual or a person or a thing.
- Those unique features or characteristics which distinguish one person or a thing from another.
- The fact that we are all not the same since we have unique traits which are innate to us. Nobody else has these traits.

This background knowledge of identity is crucial to our understanding of who we are, and subsequently, what we are on this earth for. There have been many attempts, particularly in our era of knowledge economy and postmodernism to try to redefine what identity is and how we fall into these various identity traps.

As human beings, we all have a fundamental identity. We will, for the purpose of developing our argument for this book, call it our earthly natural identity. Thus, as people living on this planet, we all have an earthly natural identity, regardless of where we live in the world. This identity is shaped/formed by the following conditions:

- *Lineage or bloodline*—this includes our parents, our tribe, clan, etc.
- *Nationality*—where we originate from in terms of geographical location or boundary. This has become fluid in recent times as a result of globalization which has brought about the movement of people between different geographical locations as a common feature.
- *Ideology / Philosophy*—what we believe in to a large extent plays a very important role in shaping our identity. An example is Feminism.
- *Sexuality*—this has become prominent in recent decades as more and more people identify themselves by their sexual orientation or preferences. The LGBTQ community is a good example of this.

In recent years, we have seen an increase in the number of emerging generation members grappling with problems of identity, and this has a ripple effect on their ability to function effectively in the world. This struggle is because there is a direct link between identity and living a life of purpose. Thus, a better understanding of this concept of identity will set the stage for a person to live life to the fullest.

Today, we find our identity from our lineage—where we come from, traced from our parents. This includes the tribe or clan we come from, our bloodline, nationality, the ideology or philosophy we subscribe to, as well as our sexuality. If you have never seen yourself through these lenses, now is the time to pause and reflect on it.

As an example, as I reflect and write this chapter, I have been amazed at the various lenses through which I see myself and my identity for that matter. For a start, I am a black person of African roots; and if I want to be precise, my roots take me to sub-Saharan Africa, West Africa to be precise. By lineage, I am both of the Ashanti and Ga tribes (parents' lineage). By nationality, I am both a Ghanaian (by birth and geographical location) and British (adoption or citizenship conferment). When it comes to ideology or philosophy, I subscribe to a worldview espoused in the Bible. I am not ashamed to subscribe and hold on to a strong Judeo-Christian worldview and it is through these lenses that I see the world around me. It is these same views that have helped shift my paradigm to that of serving humanity with the principles of the Kingdom of God. And in terms of gender, I believe that humanity was created male and female. In regard to sexuality, to ensure that we are procreating as God intended at the beginning of creation, there must be the sexual union between a man and a woman for that to happen. This is realized within the sanctity of a marriage between a husband and wife. This is how the Creator established natural laws for humanity to increase in number and to dominate the earth.

At this point, I want you to pause reading the book and reflect on the various ways by which you see your identity. Make a note of it by writing it down somewhere you can dip into now and again for reference.

Apart from our earthly natural identity, there is also a *new spiritual identity*. This has nothing to do with one's lineage or ideology or sexuality or anything like that. In fact, the Bible mentions this new identity and the fact that it is not connected to any of the factors which determine our earthly, natural one. John, one of the disciples of Jesus Christ, hints at the new identity when he wrote to testify about Jesus:

> *"He was in the world, and though the world was made through him, the world did not recognize him. He came to that which was his own, but his own did not receive him. Yet, to all who did receive him, to*

those who believed in his name, he gave the right to become children of God—children born not of natural descent, nor of a human decision or a husband's will, but born of God."

John 1:10-13 (NIV)

This scripture points to a new identity, one that is not based on our earthly one. It is an identity which is borne neither out of a husband's will nor a human decision nor of natural descent. Rather, it is an identity which is based on faith in the finished work of Jesus Christ. When Jesus Christ came into the world, humanity had lost its dominion and with it, its purpose. It had lost the original mandate God gave mankind through our forefather Adam and Eve. It had lost the original mandate it was given at creation—the mission of exercising dominion over God's creation. With the entrance of sin in the world, humanity lost its ability to function at the highest level as originally envisaged by our progenitor. With this fall from grace, it became apparent that our earthly identity was no longer enough to guarantee our effectiveness in fulfilling our assignments in the world. This ineffectiveness is still an ever-present feature in our everyday experience—and perhaps a reminder of how inadequate we are when it comes to living in our earthly identity alone.

For many an emerging generation, it creates a deep sense of loss, frustration, and the continued lack of satisfaction and fulfillment in their lives. And in a bid to numb this sense of loss of direction and clarity, they try many sensual pleasures as well as many other things to try to fill the void created by the loss. Unfortunately, this has left them in the same condition, especially of the heart. In some cases, people are worse off than they were prior to these experiments.

On the other hand, our new identity which is spiritual has the power to make up for the flaws in our earthly one. It is the identity that enables us to rise up from the ashes and be effective in our world as we seek to serve our generation. This new identity is empowering and uplifting and therefore something that is worth searching and pursuing with every fiber of our being. With it, we are able to get a new lease of life and that enables us to operate effectively at the highest level of purpose. And most importantly, it helps in answering the question of who we are and what we have been put on the earth to do. This is because among other things, our identity tells us that:

- We are a new creation, however old or young we might be. Thus, one could be seventy years old and still be a new creation. This is very important to know since our new identity is not based on our age, lineage, or bloodline (2 Corinthians 5:17).
- Our new identity displaces the old one, which has seen us become ineffective in our assignments God gave humanity at the beginning of creation—the mandate of exercising dominion over the earth domain for him. With this, we can recalibrate and recapture our original life to ensure that we are operating at full capacity which brings glory and honor to him (Genesis 1:26-28; 2 Corinthians 5:17).

Thus, our earthly identity, while it helps in establishing who we are in our interactions with the world, is ineffective in helping us answer the fundamental question of who we are and more importantly, what we have been put on this earth to do. We are always going to fall short when we operate in our earthly identity, because as good as it is, it is also flawed and inadequate.

By contrast, our new spiritual identity empowers us to understand who we truly are and from this position of understanding, we are enabled to step into our true purpose.

A fundamental grasp of this will help us serve our generation in the most effective, efficient, and productive way. In this way, when it's all said and done, like David, we will have discharged our mandate before we *see corruption*—a timely reminder of the inevitability of death and hence the need to be about our father's business!

Our new identity relies heavily on the finished work of Jesus Christ on the cross at Calvary, and our faith in what he did. A recognition that our earthly identity was not or is not sufficient enough to enable us to operate in our true purpose is fundamental. Rather than anything else, it actually derailed our quest for clarity in purpose for our life. Throughout biblical times, we see this play out time and time again. The covenant that God made with man that ensured we were walking in our true calling every time was broken and had been broken ever since—right with Adam at the genesis of creation.

Jesus Christ was God's answer to mending that broken covenant and reinstating our position in the world again. And he did this by sacrificing his life for us so that he might give his life as a ransom to us. As hinted, sacrificing his life on the cross on Calvary ensured that our brokenness was mended again—giving us a new lease of life to operate at the level God originally intended when he created us in his image and likeness. This sacrificial act restored our identity and with it answered the question of who we are and what we have been born to do.

Simply put, we have been born or created to reflect God's nature and glory on the earth, and we do that by serving and building each other up. This is the whole purpose of humanity. This is what it was when we were created for and this is what we will continue to live for.

The good news about it is that you do not need to pay any money or perform any elaborate rituals to enter into this new identity. This was our identity at creation! All you need to do is to believe that such an event happened—that is, Jesus Christ died on the cross. He died so that you can have that identity back, and more importantly, to help answer those nagging questions of identity and purpose.

To support this new life, there are a few references in the Bible that establish this new identity:

> *"He came to that which was his own but his own did not receive him. Yet to all who did receive him, to those who believed in his name, he gave the right to become children of God—children born not of natural descent, nor of human decision nor a husband's will, but born of God."*
>
> John 1:11-13 (NIV)

> *"If you declare with your mouth, 'Jesus is Lord,' and you believe in your heart that God raised him from the dead, you will be saved. For it is with your heart that you believe and are justified, and it is with your mouth that you profess your faith and are saved."*
>
> Romans 10:9-10 (NIV)

> *"Therefore, if anyone is in Christ, he is a new creation; the old has gone, the new has come."*
>
> 2 Corinthians 5:17 (NIV)

Knowing your God-given identity gives you validation and increases your faith. By this, you know that you are already equipped to do what God has called you to do, and you have faith that He will do the work through you.

Additionally, your new identity enables you to redefine who you are. With that process, comes the unravelling of your God-ordained purpose as the Bible rightly points out in Romans:

> *"Therefore I urge you brothers and sisters, in view of God's mercy, to offer your bodies as a living sacrifice, holy and pleasing to God—this is your true and proper worship.*

> *"Do not conform to the pattern of this world, but be transformed by the renewing of your mind. Then you will be able to test and approve what God's will is—**his good, pleasing and perfect will**."*
>
> Romans 12:1-2 (NIV, emphasis added)

Thus, a confession of your faith in the finished work of Jesus Christ on the cross at Calvary immediately grafts you into God's family and with it, your identity is revealed and restored. This is your identity that is not patterned along the prevailing culture of the age, but rather one that is molded on the original plan at creation. With it comes a new sense of purpose and meaning in life—*good, pleasing, and perfect* at that.

As you read this book, you have a unique opportunity to tap into this new identity. With it, you also get answers to the burning questions about life's purpose. The great news out of all this is that you get to start the journey right now, right this minute. A simple prayer or confession to God is all you need.

As simple as this prayer or confession is, it needs to come straight from the heart. You need to come to the point of saying this is it for me—a new chapter in my life, one that will enable me to have clarity in the direction of my life. If you are not there yet, I will recommend you skip this session and continue reading and learning from this book. You can always come back to this session as a way of finishing the book. But if you are serious about this prayer of confession and the commitment involved in taking this leap of faith and you are ready to say this simple prayer with purpose and meaning—coming straight from your heart—then you can repeat it as you read it, either aloud or softly, or whichever way suits you:

> Jesus, I thank you for what you did on the cross at Calvary. You were crucified there especially for me. You did this so that I can have my identity back; the identity you originally gave me when I was formed in your image and likeness. Even

though I lost it through sin (me missing the mark of your purpose in my life), you fought very hard to restore it to me even if it meant being nailed to a cross.

I ask today, as I read this book, that you restore my new identity to me. I ask that you show me what you want me to do with this new identity—you show me through this new identity who I am and what you have placed me on earth to do. This is so that I can live the rest of my life with purpose and direction. I ask that when I can't seem to find my way clearly, that you shine your light to guide my path so that I can truly live out the rest of my life in a way that is pleasing to you.

Thank you once again for the sacrifice you made for me. Today, I choose to believe that you did it for me because you love me and want the best for me. I will continue to confess your Lordship over my life as you continue to order my steps in you and as I live out a life of purpose. In your precious name I pray. AMEN!!

If you have sincerely prayed this simple prayer, words to help you articulate how you feel about where you are and more importantly, where you are going, then this marks a turning point in your life. This is what is referred to as being born again. As the earlier scriptural reference points out, this new birth is not the result of a husband's will or your parent's decision to give birth to you. Rather, this is a spiritual birth which will have a huge impact on the rest of your earthly life.

You now have a new identity: one that enables you to live a purposeful life, which among other things, empowers you to serve your generation.

I am really excited for the next chapters of your life. As you continue to read this book, you will be able to learn how you can live out the rest of your life in abundance through God by serving others. I will also encourage you to share your experience reading this book with your friends you think might be on the same journey as you.

This way, you will all journey together, encouraging and spurring on each other to greater things.

Chapter Six:
What Do I Have to Serve My Generation?

A Psychologist was giving a presentation to an audience of curious minded, motivated people on a winter's evening. The seminar, mundane as it was, was special because he used the occasion to inspire his audience, many of whom were part of the emerging generation. He used the occasion to birth forth a passion in his captive audience. He inspired their exploration of the latent power residing in the deep recesses of people.

During the presentation, he took his audience on a whistle tour of the magnificent structure they were sitting in. It was an extraordinary building, judging by the look and feel of it, not to mention the incredible attention to detail. Looking at the designs, the way it all worked; those huge beams that held it all together and how they magically stretched all the way across the expanse of the ceiling, they were all in awe of this architectural masterpiece. He drew their attention to how high the walls were. They also noticed how warm it was inside, despite the cold outside. Indeed, the design of the place met both their appreciation of beauty and their need for protection from the weather—as they all felt safe and warm. Not one of them was worried that the building was going to fall down in the middle of the seminar.

The audience at the seminar and the presenter took a moment to revel in the structure they had somewhat ignored all day. It truly was something to behold! Then the seminal moment came when he asked his captive audience about the origin of this magnificent building they were seated in. In other words, he wanted to find out if they knew where the idea for the arena came from.

Some said a builder built it, while others shouted that someone designed it before it was built, obviously! He reiterated the validity of their answer—that a designer put together into a blueprint what they hoped will be a great place, and then the building firm turned the concept on paper into a tangible space that people can see, feel, and experience.

However, he told them that what they were seeing, touching, and feeling came from an invisible world. In fact, it came from the invisible world of a toddler's soul. This seemed to baffle his audience a little bit as they struggled to come to terms with the fact that this beautiful building come from a child. He continued...

This visible arena in which they were sitting in and enjoying its warmth, protection, and security, came from the invisible soul of a twenty-month old child who we will call Jenny.

One day many years ago, Jenny, having just learned how to walk, was exploring her world more and more. She was in her play den one evening right before bedtime, getting in the last few minutes before mummy tucked her into bed, when something happened. She took a few blocks of wood, and instead of her normal pounding them down and throwing them about, she stacked one on top of another and they stayed. Then she took another block and placed it on top of the second one, and it stayed there too. As she stacked the fourth block, something leapt inside her. She felt excitement and the sheer joy on her face said it all. She laughed and exclaimed *Yay*! She was so excited to see that a tower of blocks could be built and stay there, one upon the other. Mummy and daddy took notice of what was happening in Jenny's world too as they clapped and shouted, "*Yay*" with words of affirmation like, "*that's so good Jenny!*" Everyone was enjoying the moment, but what was really happening was much more than just a moment of joy.

It was a miracle. For Jenny was discovering two of the most powerful forces in the universe—*talent* and *desire*. She found out that when she worked with blocks, whether with wood or plastic, something inside of her felt alive and filled her with joy as she desired to do it more. She added another block and when it fell, she did not quit. She built her tower over and over again—laughing, giggling, and exclaiming with each repetition of her creation. Her parents shared in her delight. Her talent for interacting with spatial design had just had its first display in the outside world.

In preschool and kindergarten, she loved the hours spent drawing and painting in art class. When she took the pencil or brush in her hand, something special happened. Not only did it provide a different level of enjoyment than running or cricket, but her teachers noticed it too. Rather than scolding her for her apathy for sports, they encouraged her with every drawing. Then she also found the same sort of attraction to her math class—an attraction which was lacking in her English literature class. Although she was good at most of her studies, math and art seemed really to give her that *"alive feeling,"* as opposed to just doing the chore of her assignments and homework. Sometimes in English class, she would find herself hiding a paper beneath her textbook on which she would draw the medieval castles described in the stories they read in class. Her parents encouraged her in her studies and praised her when she did well. When she struggled, they took the time to help her. They enforced their *'homework first and play later"* rule. The discipline they provided was becoming part of her, for when she went to university and was away from them, she studied while others partied. As a result of her hard work and diligence, she graduated with honors, becoming what she had dreamed of becoming since secondary school—*an architect*.

This character trait of determination carried on into her adult life. After being diligent and creative in her early jobs doing basic drafting and small buildings, she was given more and more responsibility. She remained faithful with her talent and had the character to bring it to fruition. Soon, she was promoted as partner at her firm, which meant a chance to do the big jobs. Her promotion came just as the city was planning a new event center, and proposal drawings were solicited.

Many more steps were involved, but in the end, Jenny's design won the bid. It was her design that created the arena where they were having the seminar on that day. It is a very interesting story, isn't it?

As beautiful as the story is, it illustrates a fundamental fact about us in our bid to serve our generation. That fact is that each and every one of us has been given something: call it a gift, an ability, a skill, natural disposition; and it is this treasure that we draw on when we serve our generation. Call them what you may, we all have all or some of these natural resources or abilities deposited inside us, waiting for our recognition so that we may better serve our generation.

David was able to serve his generation at the time because he had these resources—*gifts, skills,* and *abilities.* There were those that had been given to him by God before he was born. There were also the ones he learned as part of his growth and upskilling for the responsibilities that were going to be placed on him. Surely, the time he spent in the wilderness caring for his family's livestock provided the opportunity to hone his stewardship skills. Later on, we know that this leadership skill which he learned from shepherding came in handy when he became the king of Israel. It is this skill that enabled him to create the atmosphere of good governance in Israel, not to forget the enormous economic benefit it brought to the nation.

In addition to having these skills, his time as a shepherd afforded him the opportunity to learn the art of warfare and military strategy. Later in his reign, he deployed this skill in embarking on a military expedition. This expedition expanded the territorial boundaries of Israel, often by conquering nations and making them vassal states. These nations, as a sign of their loyalty to their conqueror, brought tributes which went into the national treasury and supported major infrastructural and developmental projects in the nation. We cannot mention David's military acumen and his skill in the art of warfare without mentioning the epic battle with the *champion of Gath,* Goliath, which announced David as the heir apparent to the throne. This seminal moment was significant as it empowered the Israelite army, who at this point had been afraid of the Philistines, to complete the rout by chasing down the Philistines and defeating them.

His love for poetry and his skill at playing musical instruments were also key in his serving of his people. As an ardent Yahwist, not only did he encourage the worship of Yahweh as an integral part of national life, he also developed musical instruments which were used in the worship of God. A study of the Psalms reminds us of his legacy, which transcends time as it forms an important part of our devotion to God (1 Chronicles 23:5; 2 Chronicles 7:6; 2 Chronicles 29:26; Amos 6:5).

All of these ways David served his generation endeared him to the people and this is why he is remembered long after his death as the greatest king Israel ever had.

We all have gifts, abilities, or what I will call natural dispositions. These are given to us at conception; whilst we were still being knitted together in our mother's womb. There are others too that we acquire as part of our education—either through formal education in the classroom or apprenticeship, or through the school of life when we go through the various phases and experiences of life. These experiences provide us with the skillset required for surviving in our environment. It is a combination of these things that equip us to better serve our generation.

To unearth these resources, we need to do the following:
- Become aware of our talents, gifts, skills, natural dispositions, desires, dreams, and other treasures in us.
- Listen to them and value them as life itself.
- Take steps to develop them beginning in very small ways.
- Seek coaching and help to make them grow.
- Do not care much about the results but just continue to express them whenever you can. Remember, you are manifesting them to help improve the lives of others and hence the need for you to continue expressing them.

Throughout the Bible, there are numerous examples of people who were endowed with gifts, talents, abilities, and skills, who deployed them for the purpose of improving the lives of the people. Here are a few examples:

> "The Word of the Lord came to me, saying, 'Before I formed you in the womb I knew you, before you were born I set you apart; I appointed you as a prophet to the nations.'"
>
> Jeremiah 1:4-5 (NIV)
>
> "But to each one of us grace has been given as Christ apportioned it. This is why it says: 'when he ascended on high, He took captives and gave gifts [spiritual] to his people. So Christ himself gave the apostles, the prophets, the evangelists, the pastors and teachers, to equip his people for works of service, so that the body of Christ may be built up until we all reach unity in the faith and in the knowledge of the Son of God and become mature, attaining to the whole measure of the fullness of Christ.
>
> "Then we will no longer be infants, tossed back and forth by the waves, and blown here and there by every wind of teaching and by the cunning and craftiness of people in their deceitful scheming.'"
>
> Ephesians 4:7-8, 11-14 (NIV)

In the Ephesians example, although the context used is for the fanning into flames of spiritual gifts, the concept holds true for all other gifts and abilities apportioned to us by our creator, the one who formed us in our mothers' wombs. Thus, we all have some natural ability seated in the depths of our soul, which society is crying out for. These gifts are there to be used in serving our generation. In this way, we can equip people for the works of service so that in the end, we, as the body of Christ, will be built up to become matured, attaining to the whole measure of the fullness of Christ. We all have the responsibility of fulfilling this mandate and the first thing we need to do is to recognize that the resource we need to do it (God-ordained assignment of service) is buried in us, simply waiting for its recognition and manifestation.

In the developmental stages of God's relationship with the people of Israel, he instructed Moses to build a tabernacle which would represent the dwelling place of his presence among his people; a constant reminder of him being their shield and exceedingly great reward. To accomplish this project, God had chosen a fine gentleman who had the skills in craftsmanship and had all the abilities needed to complete the building of the dwelling place for God. *Bezalel* was his name. This is how God described him in the Bible:

> *"Then the Lord said to Moses, 'See, I have chosen Bezalel son of Uri, the son of Hur, of the tribe of Judah, and I have filled him with the spirit of God, with wisdom, with understanding, with knowledge and with all kinds of skills—to make artistic designs for work in gold, silver and bronze, to cut and set stones, to work in wood and to engage in all kinds of crafts."*
>
> Exodus 31:1-5 (NIV)

Apart from Bezalel, God also provided skilled and gifted men who would help with the task of building the tabernacle. Chief among them was Oholiab, who was the co-builder and project manager. Oholiab was not an ordinary man; he was also a skilled gentleman like Bezalel:

> *"Moreover, I have appointed Oholiab son of Ahisamak, of the tribe of Dan, to help him. Also I have given ability to all the skilled workers to make everything I have commanded you."*
>
> Exodus 31:6 (NIV)

Bezalel is the prototype of a skilled person. He is the epitome of a life that is deposited with so much from God. When the need arose for the tabernacle to be designed and built, God activated Bezalel with those inherent skills of craftsmanship to accomplish the task. He also provided him with the men who would help complete the project since there was no way he could have completed it single-handedly. The men were equally skilled and understood the enormity of the task ahead, and were ready to deploy their gifts and talents. Later on, through the rest of Exodus, we see how Bezalel and Oholiab and the skilled men went about constructing the tabernacle, brick by brick with great attention to details. Interior design and decoration, stone masonry, gold and silver smithing, and carpentry are a few of the skills which were on display on the project.

So how do we unearth the treasures buried inside us so that we can serve our generation? How do we make sure that we are in a position to serve our generation with what we have been endowed? One thing is certain and that is that it would be a shame to live our entire lives not being able to be solution carriers and problem solvers; not being able to leave our footprints on the sands of posterity. We therefore have a duty to make sure that our society is improved, however small or big the improvement is, through our service.

So how do we do just that?

Fundamentally, we can identify the treasures we have when *we dig them up*! This will ensure that we are aware of what we have, and having identified them, use them to serve.

Dig It Up

We have seen how the visible world is brought into being by the invisible world. It is what we don't see—those latent gifts, imaginations, and abilities that give birth to what we see in the natural, material world. We are also aware that as human beings, we all have something woven into the fabric of our being, which is the medium through which we are able to bring forth into the physical world all the things of wonder, like the magnificent event center referenced earlier.

However, for us to even identify these treasures, we need to dig them up. This is a very important step. Digging them up will enable us to acknowledge their existence; with that we can serve our generation by the will of God. It is often said that the poorest person is usually not the one who has no money and other material possessions. Much as these possessions are important as they help make live pleasurable and comfortable, they are not a reflection of true wealth and worth. They are temporary and fleeting.

Rather, the poorest person is the one who does not know what they have buried inside them: those invisible traits, abilities, natural dispositions, gifts, talents, and skills. These are the mark of true wealth. With these gifts, one can create environments and things that transform people and communities. From these transformations, they get the material things that make life simple and comfortable. Such people (the poorest), even if they know what is inside of them, choose to ignore these resources as they tend not to see the importance and value in harnessing them for the greater good. Like Esau, they would rather sell their birthright (the treasures) for a bowl of some lentil soup, rather than asserting their rights by harnessing and making good use of these God-given treasures (Genesis 25:33-34).

Remember that the world is eagerly awaiting the manifestation of what you have been given, so that people can be encouraged to contribute to their community in the same way as you do when you deploy the treasure in you. This might seem surprising but that is what happens when we heed to the call to serve our generation. We, in the process, empower other people to also pluck up the boldness and confidence to step out into the unknown and create an environment that will foster the development of our fellow humans. What you have inside of you is exactly what someone out there in the world is waiting for in order for them to step into their destiny. Your lack of awareness of this right now is depriving someone from accessing the result of your treasure in order for them to move forward on their life's journey.

David was able to identify his treasures. His time with his father's sheep in the desert provided him with the skills he would later need in his reign as one of the most successful kings. These skills also unearths his flair for writing amazing poetry as an expression of his worship to God. This is evidenced in some of the greatest pieces of literary work written in human history. In addition to that, he was also musically gifted. Such was the level of his giftedness that he was able to soothe King Saul when he had periods of depression.

Could you also be very gifted with the natural disposition for music? Or have the flair to lead people into moments of worship when you play an instrument like the harp, piano, or saxophone like David did? Could you be a person who has the natural flair for Godly wisdom, that every word that comes from your mouth is seasoned with so much Godly wisdom that everybody stops in their tracks to listen to what you have to say? Could you, like Jenny, have the natural disposition to visualize a concept for a building? She brought that talent to the physical realm for the benefit and enjoyment of people—providing shelter and accommodation for people to work and dream.

The answer to these questions lies in the digging! So how do we dig the treasures up? How do we know what we have been given so that we can manifest these treasures for the betterment of our generation and society in general?

Seek the One with the Blueprint

When a product manufacturer launches a product, an important aspect of the product is the manual. It contains steps and directions on how to get the best out of the product. It also gives you indicators to what might be wrong with the product when you see it display certain characteristics. Such is the importance of the manual—that you cannot really enjoy the product until you have read the manual to help you set it up properly. It contains the manufacturer's vision for the product. It also contains the manufacturer's guarantee to you of how to get the best out of the product you have purchased.

Similarly, we are all the product of an invisible, good, creative God who molded us in his image and likeness. This is in contrast to the prevailing rhetoric which suggests that we are products of evolution and not as species created by an intelligent God. We have been deliberately, intentionally, and intricately formed by a Creator who wanted to manifest a human species that would carry his creative DNA and would eventually use the DNA to create and live in a world that reflects his creativity. We have evidence of this at the beginning of creation when we see him use the power of words (invisible) to create the world (visible) that we have today, including the pinnacle of his creation—*you and I* (Genesis 1-2).

Therefore, when we get to the point of trying to identify the DNA we carry, the best place to find it is to go to the source of it—God Almighty. And he promises us that when we come to him, he will not deny us. Rather, he will show us what we are made of and more:

> *"This is what the Lord says, he who made the earth, the Lord who formed it and established it—the Lord is his name. 'Call to me and I will answer you and tell you great and unsearchable things you do not know.'"*

Jeremiah 33:2-3 (NIV)

There are great and unsearchable things we do not know because of our limitations and frailties as human beings. Only God knows! And he bids us to come to him so that he may make known to us what his purposes for our lives are. He wants us to know what he has deposited in us to help us on our journey of discovery, and how to use these resources to serve people in our generation. All we have to do is approach him and he will show us. So will you approach him today as you read this book? If you do, he will surely answer you by unveiling his plans for your life. Ask him today, because when you ask him, you receive; when you knock on his door, he opens. When you seek, you will find, because he will show you (Matthew 7:7-8).

Become aware of these treasures—gifts, talents, dreams, desires etc.

When your intelligent creator has showed you the blueprint of your life, the onus is on you to identify them and become aware of them. This is sometimes easier said than done. One of the fundamental questions that many an emerging generation asks is: what they are good at or what they have been born to do. Now, while there may not be a one-size-fits-all answer to these questions, there are a couple of signs or hints that will indicate what you are very good at or naturally disposed to do.

Call them nudges or hints, these questions will point you in the right direction of discovery:

- *What are my strengths?*
- *What am I passionate about?*
- *What do I have (skills and resources). This will indicate the problem you were called to solve.*
- *What gives me satisfaction and fulfillment in my life?*
- *What do I enjoy doing for hours without remuneration?*

A true God-given talent will *possess* you to the point of doing that thing over and over even if there is no physical or material reward. The God who sees you in your raw state will compensate for you in more ways than you can imagine. All you need to do is to do it.

Listen to Them and Value Them as Life Itself

Remember that these questions are there to help you on the journey of discovery, which will prepare you to serve people of your generation. They are the resources that will bring you into contact with people. Therefore, it is very important that you listen and value these hints just as you value your life. That's because these treasures are life to those who pay attention to them. Continue to answer the questions above; continue to listen to those inner nudges, for these are the springboard for the discovery of what lies inside of you –the resources which will be harnessed and used in serving your generation.

Take Steps to Develop Them, Beginning in Very Small Ways

Nurturing is an important step in the process of identifying and deploying our treasures to serve people in our generation. Nurturing and developing our resources involve enrolling in various courses to sharpen and refine them for use. Jenny's flair for spatial design was followed by a stint in graduate school where she honed on her natural talent, ending up with a skill for drawing and conceptualizing buildings.

A person who has a natural disposition for singing may take singing lessons with a voice coach who can help them hone on their gift. It might also mean finding places and avenues where you can develop your skills on the job. Volunteering is one great way of nurturing a talent or skill. When I finished my teacher training, I volunteered at a night class for asylum seekers who needed to learn English as part of their integration into British society. Although I was not paid for it, I thoroughly enjoyed the experience, as it gave me the opportunity to further develop my teaching skills.

Seek Coaching and Help to Make Your Talents Grow

Part of developing the treasures you have buried inside of you is seeking the help of an expert coach. Some of the treasures can be enhanced by activating them in the right environment, such as volunteering. There are, however, those that would need the help of subject matter experts (SMEs). While some of the services of these experts are expensive, there is also good quality coaching available for lower fees. Either way, you should be prepared to put your money where your mouth is.

Researching to find out these resources has never been easier than it is today with a click of a mouse or on your mobile device—Google!

So, it is not entirely true that you don't have anything with which to serve your generation. You have been carrying within you all the resources you need to help impact the lives of people in your world—your family, community, and the world at large, one person at a time.

What is required now is to start on that journey of discovery. And as the saying goes—*a journey of a thousand miles begin with the first step.*

The first step is to seek clarity as to your potential from the one who created you and has the blueprint for your life available. Remember that when you ask you will receive; you will receive great and mighty things you do not know. Because God will download his DNA together with the treasures he has placed inside you. This will help you on the journey. He has a huge stake in you manifesting your abilities for the improvement of humanity.

Then listen to the hints and nudges and deploy them in whatever shape or form you can, one small step toward improving the lives of other people. You will also need to invest your time, energy, and money, as well as other resources to develop and hone the treasures.

You owe it to your generation and for posterity!

This is how you serve the people in your generation by the will of God so that by the time you see *corruption*, you would have left an indelible mark on humanity.

Chapter Seven: Who Do I Serve with What I Have?

David lived in a historical time of massive upheaval in Israel. Still, in the experimental stages of carving their own sovereign path away from the protection of Yahweh. They had a lot of difficult path to navigate.

To start with, there was the constant war with the Philistines with what seemed like no end in sight. In the various encounters they had with them, the Israelites were inadequate to face their arch-enemy had it not been for the intervention of God, who, prior to this, had been their ultimate shield and defender under a theocratic system of governance.

Furthermore, with the demand for a monarchy and the subsequent rejection of God, they had begun to flirt with secularism (1 Samuel 8) when the elders approached Samuel to find a suitable king for them as part of their demand for a change in direction and leadership. They were, in effect, signaling their desire to be *"like all the other nations"* (1 Samuel 8:20 NIV) without pouring over the ramifications of such demand. In the end, they got their wish, but everything went downhill from that point on.

Israel lost its place as a feared nation because of the person who had been leading them before their downhill spiral. They became a nation of ridicule as neighboring nations began confrontations because they were no longer a force to reckon with. A case in point was the encounter with the Philistines at which the sheer presence of Goliath was enough to strike fear in them. Simply put, Israel was like *a rudderless ship.*

It was during these uncertain and challenging times when the people needed someone to rise to the occasion and save Israel's blushes that David came on the scene. Equipped with the skill for the art of war, he confronted what seemed unable to be confronted, and prevailed over him with a sling and a stone. The rest, as they say, is history. It is, however, worth pointing out that armed with what he had been gifted with, David as a military leader and later as a king, served his generation, Israel. And as a result of his dedicated and excellent service, he was revered as one of the greatest kings who reigned, if not the greatest. Even though we talk about him now and will probably do that for the unforeseeable future, the fact remains that he served the generation of *his* time.

This helps us answer our own questions about who we serve with what we have. If we acknowledge that as human beings, we all have an innate ability, natural disposition, talents and skills, then the next step is to identify those we have been given the privilege to serve with what we have.

Bear in mind that a life of success (however we choose to define success) is about the positive impact we have on the lives of the people we come into contact with rather than how much wealth or material things we were able to accumulate. During his earthly ministry, Jesus warned us about giving too much credence to our earthly acquisitions as though that is the only thing we live for. He said,

> *"'Watch out! Be on your guard against all kinds of greed; life does not consist in an abundance of possession.'"*

Luke 12:15 (NIV)

The greatest among kingdom-minded people are those who serve and who do so with a spirit of excellence as it represents the heart of God.

So, who do we serve with what we have? Who have you been commissioned to serve with what God has deposited in you?

The answer is simple and complicated at the same time.

We Are Not Called to Serve All People

The truth of the matter is that although we are endowed and enabled to serve people, you and I are not called to serve all people. If it were so, we would be spreading ourselves thin and this will make us less effective in the pursuit of our assignment. A good illustration of this is in the world of business and entrepreneurship. Both are there to solve a problem or a human need.

Business entities and entrepreneurs create or develop products and services with target consumers or customers in mind. They do not create products or services for the general population. If they did this, they will end up not necessarily meeting the need of a section of the population which is their mandate. Businesses and entrepreneurial endeavors are formed and set up to spot a gap in the market and to come up with solutions to those problems or needs. This is the marketing explanation of this. What this means pretty much is that businesses and people with entrepreneurial spirit identify a need or a problem in the society; this might be among a session of society rather than the whole population. Having identified the need, they need to come up with products, goods, and services which solve the problem they identified in the first place.

This leads to some sort of market segmentation or fragmentation. In business, this is called a *niche*—a specific group of people or a specific section of the society who are most likely to identify with the product or service because it helps to solve their need. It is when a business or entrepreneur identifies their target market that they are then able to place their product or service at the location they (end users or customers of the products or service) are likely to see. This is what we ought to do and do in abundance if we are going to find and serve those we have been sent to serve.

Indeed, in our study of the life of David in the Bible, David served his own generation by the will of God. The people that David served during his time in Israel were people who had specific sets of challenges and difficulties, many of which we have highlighted at the beginning of this chapter:

- Dealing with the fallout from the failure of the first king of Israel under a monarchy: Saul.
- Facing constant threats from neighboring nations, especially the Philistines, who were a constant thorn in their flesh.
- Navigating a world where God was no longer at the center of their national life as well as personal lives with the shift from theocracy to monarchy.
- The leadership gap that was created as a result of not having anyone who was credible enough and, more importantly, approved by God to take over the reins from Saul. This leadership role was more than being on the throne. They were there to inspire confidence in the people, especially when they went to war.

You had an entire generation of people eagerly waiting for someone who would inspire confidence again, and if it was at all possible, bring God back to the heart of the national life again. This was the generation David came to serve. It was the perfect opportunity and the people that God had anointed David to serve. It was those teething problems that David was anointed to solve. And judging from what he did, it is fair to say that he did an excellent job even with the moral failings he had. And such was the level of his service that God described him as *"a man after my own heart"* (Acts 13:22 NIV). This presents a very important lesson for us as we endeavor to serve.

We Must Understand the Factors That Have Shaped Them

Part of identifying those we have been called to serve with what we have been given is understanding the factors and environment that have shaped them so that we can be able to offer answers to those challenges. This will include, among other things, how they think, what cultural, political, socio-economic and technological environments they live in and how these have shaped the way they live and think.

Armed with this background knowledge, one is more likely to have a greater impact on their target audience as a result of taking the time and efforts to know what's shaped their lives than not doing anything and expecting to make any headway in reaching and having an impact. That would be counterproductive. With the message and the medium, you are certain to reach your audience and then add value to them by serving them in whatever you have been gifted to do.

In a lot of ways, this book is written with a mission in mind: to reach out to the emerging generation, people between the ages of eighteen and forty, who might be in the middle of finding their purpose and true self-worth against the backdrop of the labels society or popular culture places on them. It is a generation that is privileged in so many ways (an example being the huge advancement in technology which has made it easier and to a large extent cheaper to be able to do great things).

Technology savvy and surrounded by enormous potential and opportunities, they are seeking for something far more eternal and fulfilling. Surely they are seeking for something beyond temporal material things. Members of the emerging generation seem to want a return to old fashion values such as integrity, ethics and morality, spirituality, equality, justice, and fairness among other virtues and not the overemphasis on sensuality, materialism, and consumerism, which is what the popular culture of today is pushing for and placing emphasis on.

To them and those who have ever wondered whether there was more to life than this, this book is written to help steer them in the right direction of finding answers. This is the reason why there is a deliberate attempt to understand the factors and environments that have shaped their paradigm, where they are likely to hang out, what questions they ask, and more. This helps in shaping the solutions we provide and how these solutions are disseminated. This is an important factor in our understanding of where they've come from.

The same can be said for all those who have served their generation and, as a result, left the world in a somewhat better place. Nelson Mandela, Mahatma Gandhi, Kwame Nkrumah, Billy Graham, and Mother Theresa just to mention a few.

Thus, as a generation, we stand the chance of changing the narrative when it comes to finding true meaning and purpose in life. The answer lies in our awareness of the treasures that are buried inside us which need to be unearthed. Once that is done, we then identify our *public,* and then we serve them with intension, passion, purpose, and excellence. This is what God empowered us to do. The question, then, is: *are you ready to heed the call?*

Chapter Eight: Where Do I Serve My Generation with What I Have?

So far on this journey of discovery, we have been reminded of who we are and what we have been placed on the earth to do. Instead of surviving and making ends meet, we have learned that we have been created to thrive on earth fashioned by a creative, intentional, and a loving father who has given us work to do—to take care of the earth and its inhabitants with Him by our side as we manage his earthly domain. In order for us to fulfill our divine assignments, he created a specie with his DNA and other traits who will exercise authority and dominion over everything he has created.

We've also learned that the best way to accomplish our divine mandate is by serving one another. This, in turn is achieved by adding value to each other and our life experiences. This is in line with our creator's desire. He demonstrated this by making the ultimate sacrifice of redeeming and reclaiming us so that we can carry on with the task assigned to us. We have learned that a life of purpose and significance is usually a life dedicated to serving our generation. In doing this, we have Jesus Christ our savior as the best example of how to do it effectively. Often laying aside his reputation and messiahship, he came to the level of humanity to demonstrate what it really meant to add value to people by serving them. The washing of the disciples' feet recorded in the Gospels is a classic example of servanthood.

We, however, do not serve in a vacuum, as we've found out in previous chapters. We have been reminded that each person has treasures buried within them which are needed to serve. This will come as a consolation to many an emerging generation, especially those who find it difficult or impossible to believe that there are treasures in them waiting to be unearthed to serve. Thus, the question of what one's life purpose is has already been answered. The answer lies in our recognition of the source of the treasures and gifts and asking him to help us identify them for the benefit of humanity. In other words, we have the answers we've been waiting for within us, begging to be discovered, so that creation will not have to wait any longer for the manifestation of God's ordained solution carriers.

This is who we are and what our divine mandate is—to manifest the Kingdom of God on earth as it is in heaven—and we get to do this by serving our generation with what we have been given. This is where we have come so far, and I'm quite sure you agree these are fundamental structures to move toward realizing our full potential for God. We do not want, under any circumstances, to fall short of our potential; what we could have achieved if we had known who we really were and what we were capable of.

Now, for us to fully step into our assignment, it's imperative that we know where to serve as we are not called to serve everybody everywhere. Trying to serve every person may not help you define your point of effectiveness. Indeed, our role model showed us where we can serve with what we have:

> *"He came to that which was his own but his own did not receive him. Yet, to all who did receive him, to those who believed in his name he gave the right to become children of God—children born not of natural descent, nor of human decision or a husband's will but born of God."*
>
> John 1:11-13 (NIV)

This principle of serving where we are needed is echoed in Matthew 9:12-13 (NIV):

> *"On hearing this, Jesus said, 'It is not the healthy who need a doctor, but the sick.'"*

In both scriptural references, Jesus demonstrates that he had come for those who believed in him as the messiah. Jesus portrays himself as the Great Physician who had come to cure the sick of their malady. In both scenarios, he paints a picture of meeting the needs of a target group rather than the whole. This is the best and most effective way we can serve our generation—going to where the needs are and meeting them.

Consequently, the most natural question to ask is where do we serve with what we have if we have not been called to serve everybody in our generation? Where do we go so that we can be the most effective? The answer is simple:

Serve Where Your Gifts Are Needed

Though a known fact but often neglected, we serve where our gifts are most needed. In such environments, we tend to flourish in our calling as our gifts are released where they are recognized, valued, and appreciated. The more they are valued, the more they are expressed for the betterment of society.

On the other hand, it will be frustrating for a gift to be expressed or manifested in a hostile environment where such precious gifts are trampled upon and despised instead of being held in high esteem. A person with such natural gifts and abilities will die inside for lack of recognition and appreciation on the part of the recipients or beneficiaries of these treasures. Though alive and active outwardly, they gradually fade away as they feel undervalued and unappreciated. This is the reason why it is vitally important that we spot someone who clearly has gifts and abilities to help them express them by creating an enabling environment which will foster the fanning into flames of these gifts and abilities.

Once again, Jesus is the best example of someone who served where his gifts and abilities were recognized and valued. During his earthly ministry, Jesus taught hundreds of people about the Kingdom of heaven. And such was the level and depth of his knowledge that his target audience recognized that he was not an ordinary man:

> "When Jesus has finished saying these things, the crowds were amazed at his teaching because he taught as one who had authority and not as their teachers of the law."

Matthew 7:28-29 (NIV)

We see in the example above when a person with a gift or ability expresses them and how its intended recipients respond. The people in the temple on that day recognized that Jesus, young as he was, had authority in what he said as they were backed by miracles such as the feeding of the four and five thousand as well as the numerous healing miracles that took place. Additionally, they recognized a depth of wisdom in what Jesus said as none of their teachers had ever expressed such thoughts.

By the same token, we also see an environment where the gifts and abilities are not appreciated and what the result of such lack of appreciation is:

> "When Jesus had finished these parables, he moved on from there. Coming to his hometown, he began teaching the people in their synagogue and they were amazed. Where did this man get this wisdom and these miraculous powers they asked? Isn't this the carpenter's son? Isn't his mother's name Mary and aren't his brothers James, Joseph, Simon and Judas? Aren't all his sisters with us? Where then did this man get all these things? **And they took offense at him.**
>
> "But Jesus said to them, 'A prophet is not without honor except in his own town and in his own home. **And he did not do many miracles there because of their lack of faith.**'"

Matthew 13:53-58 (NIV, emphasis added)

In this story, people who knew Jesus not only despised his God-given ability but also took offense that he dared express those abilities. To make matters worse, he, by virtue of his lineage or townsfolks, was not meant to have such eloquence, wisdom, and boldness to communicate such messages never heard in the town until then. He also had the power to heal people of their problems!

This, rather than exciting them, infuriated them. And the result? Well, they were not able to receive the benefits of the gifts because of their attitude. This should remind us not to despise the gifts people carry. We stand to miss out on the blessing and benefit of their expression when we despise them. In the end, Jesus went to places where his gifts were appreciated and valued and there, there were many miracles and his brand of wisdom got the best reception.

When a gift is needed, it is often recognized, valued and appreciated. This is where we must serve with what we have.

Serve Where Your Gifts Are Celebrated

Finding a space where your gifts are appreciated and celebrated is very important as it gives credence to your passion in seeing humanity become all that God created it to be. When your gifts are celebrated, it means that the beneficiaries recognize your role in changing their narrative and you become very much a part of their journey. Does that mean you should only go to such environments? Remember Jesus from the previous scriptural references, because his gifts and abilities were not celebrated, limited his ability to help change their narrative and hence the reason why he was wasn't able to do any miracles.

Possibly with such attitude, the people will have despised something spectacular or worse still, the miracles wouldn't have had the desired impact on the people.

We also see on other occasions in Scripture that when his gifts and abilities are recognized by the number of people who pushed through to hear him speak as well as demonstrate his divine power and authority in miraculous signs, he was able to thrive and do amazing things. The people were hungry for more of such demonstrations. The lesson here is that though the world is our stage to manifest our God-given abilities, such manifestations turn to accomplish their desired effect when they are appreciated and valued by those for whom it was intended.

We have a great part to play in releasing people into their destinies. Without a doubt, it is God who births in people the desires, abilities, and gifts, but we also augment the process by creating the environment for people to flourish in unearthing them and serving humanity with them. Additionally, we can also support them to carry out their divine mandate both spiritually by praying for them and physically, encouraging them, especially during the challenging times of their lives. This way, we will be fulfilling God's commands of loving and encouraging one another as Christ demonstrated during his life on earth.

So, where else can you serve with what you have been given? What environments will help nurture those gifts and abilities while you add value to humanity at the same time? Well, there are a lot of places and environments that need your God-given resources for such environments to thrive.

Local Communities

It is often said that charity begins at home, and this could not be more timely when it comes to where one can serve with what they have. There is a whole world out there waiting for our gifts and abilities, and this makes us want to jump on a plane and fly out to remote and less-developed parts of the world where we truly feel help is needed the most. Now, while this is a very noble and laudable idea, it is worth looking around our neighborhoods and communities for the need present nearby. This tends to happen in more affluent and developed parts of the world. But for these parts, there are a lot of things going on that need our urgent attention. Help your community thrive.

While on the subject, I am reminded of the chorus of one of the songs of one of the contemporary gospel group, Casting Crowns. It simply says if we want to see change in the world out there, then it's got to start right here at home, and start right now! Begin serving humanity where you are and then *from there* you can transform your country or the world in general.

Volunteering your time, resources, and services frequently is all that is required to serve your generation. Mentoring and buddying members of the emerging generation is the right place to start. As you listen to these future leaders share their pain, frustrations, and aspirations for the future, you can help encourage and shore up their confidence for a brighter future simply by being there for them and loving them as Jesus would. You don't need to know all the answers to life's questions. They often need to know God loves them and has given them specific traits to provide something unique to his Kingdom.

Church Setting

In the early days of the church—the gathering of God's called people—there was an incident that took place which highlights how relevant the church was back then and is today. It also reiterates the importance of deploying our skills and gifts to serve in that environment. This is how the story is recorded in the book of Acts:

> *"In those days when the number of disciples was increasing, the Hellenistic Jews among them complained against the Hebraic Jews because their widows were being overlooked in the daily distribution of food. So the Twelve gathered all the disciples together and said, 'It would not be right for us to neglect the ministry of the word of God in order to wait on tables. Brothers and sisters, choose seven men from among you who are known to be full of the Spirit and wisdom. We will turn this responsibility over to them and we will give our attention to prayers and the ministry of the word.'*
>
> *This proposal pleased the whole group, they chose Stephen, a man full of faith and of the Holy Spirit; also Philip, Procorus, Nicanor, Timon, Parmenas and Nicolas from Antioch, a convert to Judaism. They presented these men to the Apostles who prayed and laid their hands on them.*
>
> *So the word of God spread. The number of disciples in Jerusalem increased rapidly and a large number of priests became obedient to the faith."*

Acts 6:1-7 (NIV)

The scene presented in the scripture above is one of chaos and confusion. It demonstrates the teething problems when God begins to birth something new. Sometimes, it can get a little messy. Do we have messy gathering of the "called ones"? Yes, we do!

But we also see an organized church at the end of the scene. The church began to grow exponentially as people created a relevant and organized home. And in the midst of the organization, the Word of God was preached with conviction and backed by the Holy Spirit, which was evident for all to see. This made the gospel attractive because of what it offered, and this enhanced the lives of those who enjoyed the benefits of their newfound faith.

We also noticed that a decision was taken to address the chaos and confusion in the church at the time. The solution was to select men of repute *known to be full of the Holy Spirit and wisdom*. I'm quite sure they were men who were also identified for their skills as well as their spiritual gifts. These were the men who were tasked with the responsibility of maintaining peace and order so that the work of advancing the gospel of Jesus Christ would continue unhindered. I have no doubt that these men served their generation with such excellence and dedication. And when they felt like giving up, they were enabled by the Holy Spirit, which they were full of to accomplish their divine assignment. And because of their work, the needs of the church were met and this enabled God through the Holy Spirit to move among the people—the evidence of which was seen by many. This led to the rapid spread of the gospel, and with it came the harvest of souls as more and more people heeded the call for repentance and salvation.

The church in this hour is a great place to serve our generation. The church of the living God in this hour is the *"pillar and foundation of the truth"* (1 Timothy 3:15 NIV). And if it is to stand and be a voice that it was created to be as evident in the early church, then it will require men and women who are not only known to be full of the Spirit and wisdom but also skilled to step up and serve their generation by helping create the environment so the holistic message of the gospel reaches the uttermost parts of the earth.

As someone who is eager to identify what they have in order to serve their generation, you also need to adopt the same mindset as the *Men of Issachar*. To give you a sense of what the mindset is about, this is what the Bible has recorded about them:

> *"Of the tribe of Issachar,* **men who understood the times** *with* **knowledge of what Israel should do,** *two hundred chiefs; and all their relatives were at their command."*
>
> 1 Chronicles 12:32 (AMP, emphasis added)

> *"From Issachar,* **men who understood the times and knew what Israel should do**—*200 chiefs, with all their relatives under their command."*
>
> 1 Chronicles 12:32 (NIV, emphasis added)
>
> *"And of the children of Issachar, which were* **men that had understanding of the times, to know what Israel ought to do**; *the heads of them were two hundred and all their brethren were at their command."*
>
> 1 Chronicles 12:32 (NKJV, emphasis added)

The men of Issachar, who were the descendants of one of Jacob's twelve sons, were noted for their knack for discerning the times they lived in. In the context of the Bible, they recognized that the time was right for them to transfer their allegiance from the house of Saul, who had been rejected by God, to David. They were able to discern the time and season for this to take place and in line with God's purpose. This recognition also helped legitimize David's throne.

I do believe we must develop and nurture the spirit of the men of Issachar—to discern the times and seasons we live in. And more importantly, identify what we must to do so that we live purposeful and intentional lives for God. Remember, we can do all things through Christ who gives us strength! (Philippians 4:13) for it is Christ who works in us both to will and to do according his good purpose (Philippians 2:13).

While modern day presents new and unprecedented challenges, it also provides a great opportunity for the church to live up to its mandate as the pillar and foundation of the truth.

The COVID-19 pandemic has required radical solutions. Over the last year and half or so, we've seen our freedoms curtailed, if not completely taken away from us, often limiting us to the bare minimum. With it have also come unprecedented economic hardships with far-reaching consequences. In these times, we've also seen people turn to various sources, including the media, for inspiration to help them survive and stay afloat. Whether what they are being fed with is wholesome is anyone's guess.

At the same time, we've also seen a hunger for truth and things that steer people in the right direction. Sadly though, many have turn to the wrong places in their quest to find what they believe will satisfy them. This is where the church comes in. The gathering of the called-out ones has a unique opportunity in this hour to propagate the truth about the gospel of Jesus Christ. That in these challenging times, humanity needs Jesus; the world needs to know that Jesus Christ is the answer to all the chaos and confusion!

Having said that, it is also reassuring to see the church rise up to take their place in a post-modern, post-Christian world and hopefully will remain pivotal in a post-COVID-19 world. We've seen the church, to some extent, forced to innovate in order to reach the world with the message of the gospel. I do believe that the church, as a result of the global health crisis, is beginning to take notice of the pivotal role it plays in bringing the world closer to God.

But how well is the church prepared for the harvest, and how prepared is the church to disciple those who come to Jesus as a result?

There will definitely be scenes reminiscent of the one we saw in the early church in the Acts of the Apostles. There will be issues of discrimination of various forms and shapes as we've already seen in recent times. In the midst of this, there will be questions about the relevance of the church in today's secular culture. There will also be welfare issues similar to the ones in the early church.

Simply put, the church is going to be messy as people come in as they are to be rescued and disciple. This will bring chaos and confusion with it. It will also be the finest hour as the Holy Spirit draws people who are known to be full of him and wisdom to plug the gap and usher in a paradigm shift.

God will stir the hearts of men and women who will step up to disciple the harvest—the growing church of God. He will raise people with varying human resource who would rise to the challenge of advancing the Kingdom of God in our culture by serving people, discipling and adding value to these precious people.

The church in this hour needs you to help reach out and be the pillar and foundation of the truth. I am so privileged to have the opportunity to serve my generation by mentoring some amazing young adults and students in the city of Cambridge and surrounding towns in the United Kingdom. Through Ignite Young Adults and Students Connect Group, I am able to deploy my experience of life and use my skillset as a teacher to encourage, inspire, and hopefully model the way to live as Christian in a post-modern world. Through this group, I have been able to serve these amazing young men and women for the past five years and still counting, and I get the greatest joy out of that.

Do I have answers to all of life's questions to be in that position? No! I don't have all the answers to life's crucial questions as I am also on the same journey of figuring out the way to live a purposeful life. Through Christ, I am able to live out my life one day at a time and the lessons I learn I pass to the people I serve and mentor. We do need more men of Issachar who understand the times we live in and are available to serve their generation. The emerging generation needs to be mentored, to be shown the way, to be guided on the path of righteousness and integrity. They are the harvest God is bringing into the church, and this will require people who are filled with the Holy Spirit and wisdom to roll up their sleeves.

The church needs people who are passionate and with the skillset to mentor and inspire the emerging generation and to equip them for life in an increasingly challenging world which places huge pressure and demands on them.

So if you want a setting or environment to serve your generation with what you have, the church is one of the environments to unleash your potential in adding value to people by serving them.

The 7 Mountains of Culture

Leading by example in the cultures you live within is another environment wherein we can serve our generation and share the gospel. This can range from one's place of employment, college or university, and their businesses as entrepreneurs (among others).

This might seem out of sync with the values and moral of Christians as mingling with the world ends up corrupting God's people and drawing them away from Him and into the hand of the enemy. Throughout the Bible, there are numerous examples of people who serve God and their generation in secular environments. The two examples that readily come to mind are Joseph and Daniel.

Joseph was the young teenager who ended up in a foreign country after been traded off by his brothers. He later ended up in the house of one of the powerful men in Egypt. Although he served his master with integrity, he ended up in prison for refusing to give in to the amorous advances of his master's wife. Through his knack for interpreting dreams, he was brought from the prison into the palaces and corridors of power in Egypt. Perhaps the highlight of his career is when he not only interpreted the King of Egypt's dreams but also provided a solution to the problem the dream recognized. This averted a catastrophic hunger in the land. Joseph later became renowned in the land because of his gifts and the life of integrity he demonstrated during those challenging times.

What Joseph did in a foreign country was serve not only his adopted country but also his fellow Hebrews. He served by identifying a problem and devising a solution to them. From his story, it is worth noting that Joseph did not serve in a church or any religious establishment. Rather, he served his generation in a *hostile* environment. And he served with his God-given gifts and abilities.

With a looming severe drought on the horizon, Joseph was able to see far ahead and anticipate what was going to happen. He recommended they store food for the drought or lean season. Using his gift of interpreting dreams, he was able to devise a strategy for food storage and preservation which ensured that there was grain for the people of Egypt when the famine eventually began. As a result of his effort, the nation of Egypt was spared the harsh hunger and thirst which followed the season of abundance and which would have otherwise decimated the land. It also ensured that a section of his family in Canaan were not wiped out as a result of starvation.

He served his generation by adding value to humanity in a place where he was meant to have been a slave. He didn't allow himself to be sidetracked by the wrongs his brothers had committed against him. Rather, he used it as a catalyst to propel him into a state of servanthood in a difficult living situation. The entire nation of Egypt came to know him for his exploit and for literally saving humanity.

Similarly, Daniel also excelled in government in a foreign land. He and four other Hebrew men displayed a high level of excellence and professionalism in the face of mounting pressure to compromise on their faith. Their level of excellence did not go unnoticed by the authorities at the time. Darius, the Babylonian king at the time, said this about the God of Daniel and the Hebrew boys:

> "Then King Darius wrote to all the nations and peoples of every language in all the earth: 'May you prosper greatly! I issue a decree that in every part of my kingdom, people must fear and reverence the God of Daniel.
>
> "For he is the living God and he endures forever; his kingdom will not be destroyed, his dominion will never end. He rescues and he saves; he performs signs and wonders in the heavens and on the earth. He has rescued Daniel from the power of the lions."
>
> Daniel 6:25-27 (NIV)

Daniel excelled where he was placed, and that influenced the culture of the country. Today, God is looking for missionaries in the marketplace who will bring salt and light to the environments with the express aim of establishing a culture that magnifies the will of God here as it is heaven. An aggressive but subtle fights over our minds, hearts, eyes, and mouths. This war threatens the very moral fabric of our society. The war is being fought on various levels and spheres that hold sway over our culture. And the levels include education, religion, family, business, government, arts, entertainment, and media.

There is a great need to send out missionaries, people full of the Holy Spirit and with wisdom and understanding, to invade these areas and wrestle back control for God.

This is why one needs to consider their present surroundings as their mission field and be intentional about saturating the environment with the principles of the Kingdom of God. When done, this will add value to humanity and will ensure that our generation is served.

Chapter Nine: Where do I Serve with What I Have?

7 MOUNTAINS OF CULTURE

My wife and I usually kick back on most Friday evenings after a full on week. We are not your average British couple in the sense that we don't go to the pub on Friday nights and weekends with the intent to get drunk. Our idea of a good night in and a great weekend is usually relaxing to a great, thought-provoking film.

We are given a huge array of options for films, though. Unfortunately, this has created a bit of a dilemma as we always struggle to find something wholesome to watch.

And just to give you an idea of what we consider to be an ideal movie to watch—it has to have a good moral story, great acting, devoid of swearing, and certainly without the raunchy sex scenes. We want a good entertainment without getting defiled and definitely not defiling our body's gates—our eyes, mouth, ears and heart! And this is where the problem begins...

These days, we are finding it incredibly difficult trying to find something decent to watch so much that on some occasions, we end up not watching anything at all and rather spending the time having meaning conversations, which I must say is more interesting and invigorating. Having great and intimate communication with one's spouse is way more precious and important in a happy and meaningful relationship and one that I cherish. I am quite sure we are not the only ones facing challenges of trying to find something decent on the various streaming platforms.

A keen observer would notice that there is the gradual chipping away of what is considered to be wholesome, decent, and morally uplifting all in the name of creativity and pushing the boundaries—a phrase commonly used by many an emerging generation of creatives.

Quite apart from innovating, these subtle changes represent a radical agenda by those gatekeepers in the industry aimed at changing the nature of one's life and what we believe. Over the years, we have seen this agenda aggressively pushed into the mainstream of national consciousness, gradually and subtly replacing good-old fashion values that have helped shape civilizations and cultures for centuries. No wonder there is a scramble to grab these key facets of our culture as whoever holds the keys to them, and by holding the keys I mean ownership, has power and control to shape our values, thought patterns, and even the narrative.

In West Africa, I studied government. It was one of my favorite subjects in school alongside economics, history, and English literature. Government as a subject focused on political theories and institutions that shaped societies and nations. So, among other things, we learned about the theory of separation of power as espoused by the French political theorist Baron de Montesquieu and how it works in Parliamentary and Presidential systems of government, as well as the rule of law, among other theories. I learned that in countries that practiced the Westminster model of parliamentary democracy, there is a fusion of powers where the three arms of government – legislature, executive and the judiciary - are not independent of each other, but rather, they are fused together as evidenced in how it operates in the United Kingdom. For instance, the British Prime Minister appoints members of his cabinet from Parliament, thus making the relationship between the legislature and executive arms of government intertwined.

I recently discovered a political drama on Netflix called *Designated Survivor*. It starred Kiefer Sutherland as a cabinet minister who becomes the president of the United States of America following a terror attack on Capitol Hill, the seat of the American legislature. This happened during the State of the Union address by the president at the time. I have since watched the series and learned that the plot is based on what happens each year at the presidential address to congress in which the president outlines the strength (or otherwise) of the union. Before the ceremony, a member of the cabinet is chosen as a designated survivor. They are taken to a secret location, away from Washington. This is to ensure the continuity of government in the event of a catastrophe that kills the president at the address. It was during one of the addresses that tragedy hit the country.

Tom Kirkman, who was the secretary for housing and urban development, was chosen as the designated survivor and ended up becoming the most powerful person on the planet.

The series takes us through his journey through the presidency and the challenges he faced both domestically and internationally. It gives an insight into the workings of a government in a modern democracy, highlighting the myriad topics and issues the president and his advisors have to deal with on a regular basis. It also shows how he balanced the role of being the president of the most powerful nation on earth with being a husband with a teenage son and a young daughter. I really enjoyed the intricacies of modern diplomacy and how to deal with the challenging political situations.

However, a few episodes into the series, I began to notice a trend which interrupted my interest in the political drama. I believe this highlights Hollywood's agenda, which is aimed at reengineering the way we think and live. In the third season, the writers introduced a sub-plot in which a young, African-American public relations advisor with expertise in social media was hired onto the presidential staff to help project the president in good and positive light after a slump in his approval ratings. Unfortunately, the gentleman who was a very handsome young man was also gay heavily involved in sexual relations with one of the president's security detail. It was at this stage that I switched off completely ending my affinity with *Designated Survivor*.

Hollywood sent me a subliminal message in that sub-plot between the two gentlemen. And the message was this; that in today's culture, this was the new normal. The impression I got was that there was an unwritten convention in the creative industry more so Hollywood that for every script developed for a movie or series, there needed to be these sorts of relationships as well as other non-traditional values written into storylines as well as plots and sub-plots as a way of reflecting society in modern times. And this is not just in the movie industry. In fact, it has already permeated other facets of modern life. One gets the sense there is a tsunami sweeping across the globe that aims to radically change the way we view ourselves and the way we live.

There are seven areas in our culture where the invasion and radical shift is most prominent. These areas represent the mirror into the soul of our modern culture and hold huge influence over our lives. A cultural onslaught is unleashed in these areas—one that we all ought to take notice. These areas are the family, religion, business and economics, politics and government, education, media, and the arts. These greatly influence our culture and our lives. And they all seem to be connected to each so that one area heavily influences the other.

These are the mediums or weapons deployed by those on top of these mountains; gatekeepers we'll call them for want of a better term to shape our culture by changing the way we see the world around us and the values that have shaped our lives which all but removes biblical or Judeo-Christian values from individual and national life. Through these mountains, humanity is gradually losing its identity as we head toward the era of moral and spiritual decadence represented in the life of the Corinthians in the New Testament and the great rebellion of Sodom and Gomorrah during the time of Nimrod.

When you take a look at these spheres (or mountains) of influence in our societies, you can see a common trend that runs through—steps that all but obliterate values and ethics that have shaped nations and cultures for centuries and generations and that are not necessarily in the best interest of humanity.

And this is where we come in! Our mandate with the seven mountains of influence is for us to reclaim them with the express purpose of bringing them under the influence of God and everything he represents. The values he left us have shaped our world for many centuries and are currently under threat from the gatekeepers of these mountains. As the emerging generation, we ought to make it our life goal to reverse the tide not only for ourselves but also for posterity.

See the invasion taking place in our homes, on our television screens and computers, in our families and education system, on the airwaves, as well as in the marketplace. Take the necessary steps to redeem our culture for God and humanity. This is the reason why all the gifts, talents, skills, and abilities you have need to be harnessed for this cause. They have a far greater purpose to serve.

But what exactly is the subtle battle going on upon these mountains? What is really happening behind the scenes or in plain sight that we don't seem to see as an onslaught? At face value, there doesn't seem to be a lot going on in our lives. If anything at all, we are enjoying the best times of our lives with wide ranges of options to choose from. To add to this, these mountains have contributed immensely in creating the lives that we want.

Now, while this might be true to some extent, there is no denying that these mountains have been hijacked and used in advancing a certain worldview diametrically opposed to the values which have shaped our lives.

Arts and Entertainment

To many, the arts and entertainment mountain is made up of idols that captivate hearts as they influence our behavior and attitude toward one another. Many an emerging generation is influenced by the music industry, for example. It plays into the soul and can open people to certain dimensions and realms of influence and control their spirits. The lyrics of some of the songs and the explicit nature of the images that accompany the songs doesn't leave much to be desired.

To add to this, Hollywood for many decades, has been at the forefront of churning out a dystopian and distorted perception about every facet of human life. They are now the gatekeepers and boundary setters when it comes to what should constitute a healthy and balanced life. Movies that project a blatant rejection of morality and good values has become the rule rather than the exception. This is why we urgently need people filled with the spirit in this sphere of influence to change the narrative and bring back morality, ethics, and good values onto our screens and in our music.

If you are a gifted musician, know that your gift is there to help create great sound and wholesome lyrics that will lead people to live godly lives. If you are aspiring to write scripts for movies, TV series, or any of the streaming service, I encourage you to write great and entertaining scripts with a lot of cliff-hanging moments but above all, the scripts should be inspired by your Judeo-Christian principles and worldview that recognizes God as the creator of the universe, including humanity; glorify God. This is why I love the Kendrick Brothers. Alex and Stephen are the brains behind such entertaining, thought-provoking, inspiring, and Bible-based films as *War Room*, *Facing the Giants*, and *Courageous*. This duo is interested in portraying life through the lens of the Bible with all the bells and whistles that comes with Hollywood. They have proved it can be done when we are passionate to serve our generation by leading them to the truth.

Family

Thanks largely to Hollywood, we have, in recent years, seen a war waged on the concept of family. The subliminal messages portrayed suggest that the family structure is undergoing a massive renovation. This has accelerated with the emergence of the LGBTQ+ community, who advocate for same rights as heterosexual couples.

Family is the first institution established by God through the covenant of marriage. One of his aims was that the family grow to become a peculiar tribe of people who are separated to be his treasured possession. This traditional concept of the family with marriage between a man and woman at the core is constantly being redefined to one that is diametrically opposite to the original plan at creation. Boundaries are being redrawn every time with the aim of making it confusing for people.

We need an army of Spirit-led men and women who will make it their life purpose in reclaiming this mountain and making it subject and obedient to the boundaries God set for mankind.

Education

The importance of education and the role it plays in the development of the human character—as well as the influence it has on our lives later on—cannot be overemphasized. This is because it the premise upon which the very essence of all our actions are formed. What we do and become is what we know and have learned. Education is a self-enlightening process, which leads to insight both spiritually and physically. It also helps to shape and build our character; it is crucial to the development of the total man.

With the influence coming from the other mountains such as the arts and entertainment industry for example, it is vital that we defend the values we input into our children by engaging with it and helping to set the agenda. This begins at home with the family.

Business and Finance

The global financial crash of 2008 provides us with sober reflection of how greed, exploitation, and lack of sympathy has fueled a business culture in which profits come before people. Shady business practices reward bad decisions, which is another issue at the heart of many businesses. The global elite control the world financial system with the strategy of controlling every institution and enslaving people into debts in the hope of increasing profit margins.

The ability to create wealth through ingenuity, enterprise, creativity, and effort is a God-given gift and a universal impulse. The markets and economic systems that emerge whenever people are free to pursue buying and selling become the lifeblood of a country. This includes farms to small businesses to large corporations.

This realm is prone to corruption through idolatry, greed, and covetousness. In response, God's people must embrace its responsibility to train up those who are called into the marketplace to manage business as well as engage in entrepreneurial endeavors geared towards the generation and equitable distribution of the wealth that come from such ventures. Additionally, God's people must provide leadership with integrity and honesty in the spheres of our culture.

As evidenced throughout the Bible, it is the Lord's will to make his people prosperous and that he desires for his church to use its wealth to finance the work of the Kingdom expansion. Simply put, the business mountain is about prosperity with a purpose.

Government

There is a certain perception particularly among Christians that suggests it is almost impossible for one to be a "good Christian" and a politician at the same time. These two do not mix just like water and oil. One always comes up to the surface. For reasons best known to people, being a Christian and a politician or being in government portrays a certain level of mistrust and skepticism as the assertion is that the policies of governments tend to go diametrically opposite to the Christian worldview held by people who practice the Christian faith.

And yet, the policies and laws enacted affects all citizens alike, Christians or otherwise. Proverbs 14:34 (NIV) states *"righteousness exalts a nation, but sin is a reproach to any people."* Many times, as exemplified in the Old Testament, a nation's moral standards are dependent on those exhibited by its leaders. While each individual is responsible for their own sins, the fact remains that people are greatly influenced by the morals that popular leaders adopt.

The progressive liberal agenda, empowered by well-known men and women in the arts and entertainment industries, have made significant gains in the political arena over the past few decades. In fact, many liberal groups seek to remove anything related to God and Christianity from governmental and education systems because of the misapplied interpretation of the phrase "separation of church and state."

We must see a shift in this arena in order to preserve the Christian heritage that most civilizations were founded upon. The goal is to put in place righteous political leaders who will positively affect all aspects of government.

Media

The media mountain includes all the gatekeepers in information dissemination. These include the various news sources such as radio, TV news stations, newspapers, internet news. and opinions sites. The media has huge potential to become a force for the good of humanity as it sways popular opinion on current issues based upon its reporting, but currently it is not always truthful and accurate. No wonder it is an industry dominated by a few barons who use these mediums to promote a certain narrative!

In some cases, they are literally the king makers – that is those who use their influence in the media to shift public opinion on who should be elected into office or in support of a particular agenda. This is very common during elections in countries. A classic example is the Murdoch media empire around the world. This empire, owned by the Australian-American media baron Rupert Murdoch, controls a large sway of media houses across the globe but mostly in western countries. In the United Kingdom, the empire includes the Sky channels, the *Times* Newspaper, the *Sun* newspaper—among others. These platforms are often used in expanding the liberal agenda, which all but obliterates Judeo-Christian views, morality, and ethics from our national consciousness.

There needs to be a rise in various media where morality and Christian values and views are brought back to the forefront of national debates and discussions once again.

However, to bring true transformation to the media mountain, Christians who are called into this industry must be willing to report righteously and truthfully in a secular marketplace.

Religion

Every society has some form of belief regarding a superior being or beings. In the east, religions tend to be polytheistic, where there are gods or outright idols, such as Hinduism and Buddhism. Although these religions are thousands of years old, they nonetheless continue to thrive today.

In the west, Christianity and Catholicism are predominant but post-modern views are increasingly being accepted and the concept of God is being rejected. This is especially true for Europe. The Christian church is described in the Greek language as the *ekklesia* (ecclesia). Literally translated, *ekklesia* means "governing body" or "the gathering of those summoned." Although theocracy, a governmental structure where a deity rules, is no more in practice in our modern culture, this translation suggests that the church should have great influence in all sphere of society.

It is the church's responsibility to reach the lost with love and the gospel of Jesus Christ and expand the Kingdom in ministerial effort both nationally and internationally.

Thus, when you look at these spheres of our culture, there is a battle fought for our minds, eyes, wallets, and families among other things. As members of the emerging generation seeking for a way to live purposefully in our culture, it behooves on us to understand the times and seasons we live in so that we are better enabled to engage these mountains with a counter-cultural mindset.

Some of you might be pursuing education in these areas at this moment. Do remember that the purpose of your studies is so you can be an agent of change in your society? To help change the narrative to one that exalts the name of Jesus above all other names as well as advocating for the reinstatement of the principles upon which our societies have been built?

We need to see ourselves as the Josephs and the Daniels of our generation who are ready to provide pragmatic solutions to the problems we face daily. Like David, we ought to be asking the question *"Is there not a cause?"* We need music writers and artistes to come up with wholesome and anointed music that glorifies God in our culture. We need emerging generation members who are passionate about creating a fair and equal society at the governmental level with such excellence as exemplified by Daniel and the four Hebrew boys.

If you are already working in any of the seven mountains or are considering a career in any of them, prayerfully consider the assignment on your life. Consider what you can and are bringing to the industry, and always remember that you are not going there to compromise or defile yourself with the portion of the king's meat (Daniel 1:8), but rather, you are there to be *light*, illuminating the dark places of the industry with the principles of the Kingdom of God. You are also there as the *salt*, bringing flavor to the place as well as help preserve the ancient landmark in those places. Selah!

Chapter Ten: When Do I Serve with What I Have?

If there was ever a time to serve our generation with what we have been given, it is now. This sounds simple, doesn't it? Once you have identified what you have been endowed with to improve humanity through value adding to life, unearth it! To quote Jesus's words, the talents buried inside you were not meant to be hidden under a bushel. Never! (Matthew 5 verse 5).

It was meant to be unearthed that humanity may be enriched. So that in the end, gratitude and honor will be given to the giver of the treasures. Once that is done, that is identifying what we have, we then move straight into serving those for whom we have been assigned as David did. He served people in his own generation.

On one hand, there is never a right time for one to serve their own generation with a sense of urgency since we will, like David, see corruption. With this, there is a sense in which we have to get down to the business of serving once we know what we have.

On the other hand, the Bible makes it clear that there is a time and season for every activity under the heavens. This is what Solomon said in the book of Ecclesiastes:

> *"There is a time for everything, and a season for every activity under heaven."*

Ecclesiastes 3:1 (NIV)

Therefore, one's effectiveness in serving their generation and its subsequent success will depend on their ability to discern the seasons and to know when to take the first step. This is crucial not only to the servant but also to the generation they are being called to. This ensures that both can reap the rewards—the servant fulfilling their purpose and the generation enriched by the treasures of the servant.

When we consider the climate we live in today, we have situations in which generation servers are needed, and they are needed now. The environment is ripe for people with a heart to impact their generation to stand up and be counted. This is what this book is written to do—to awaken giants with a heart to serve their generation by deploying their skills and gifts in adding value to humanity. There is a sense in which time is running out for this current generation. We have a window of opportunity to execute the assignment on our lives, for it is only when we do this that we'll find meaning and purpose to our lives.

As a generation server, you owe it to the emerging generation in your city, community, and country to help them see who they really are and the battle going on for their hearts and minds, a battle represented by the seven mountains of influence in our culture covered in the previous chapter. We learned about their subliminal but devastating agenda to change the narrative about how to live our lives. This is the reason why the time to serve our generation is now!

In serving your generation, you must be prepared to stay the race with a high level of enthusiasm and passion. You have to commit yourself to working tirelessly and most importantly, with the help of the Holy Spirit to go as far as you can go before you see corruption. Solomon again reiterates the importance of staying the course of an endeavor even when you don't see any positive sign of progress:

> "Whoever watches the wind will not plant; whoever looks at the clouds will not reap.
>
> "As you do not know the path of the wind or how the body is formed in a mother's womb, so you cannot understand the work of God.
>
> "Sow your seed in the morning and at evening, let not your hands be idle, for you do not know which will succeed, whether this or that or whether both will do equally well."

Ecclesiastes 11:4-6 (NIV)

In this passage, Solomon advises us not to throw in the towel when we don't see any fruit of our labor. The secret to success is in persevering in sowing your seeds and not letting your hands be idle because you don't see any sign of harvest. The harvest eventually comes when we stay the course. Keep sowing and watering the seed.

This is the attitude we need to develop if we are going to fulfill our assignment in serving our generation and do so successfully. You may be shouting on the rooftop and yet not getting through to your target group. For this, you must follow Jesus' example and keep serving. Keep positioning yourself intentionally with the aim of serving until you see corruption. Jesus did the same during his sojourn on earth:

> *"He came to that which was his own but his own did not receive him. Yet to all who did receive him, to those who believed in his name, he gave them the right to become children of God—children born not of natural descent, nor of human decision or a husband's will but born of God."*

John 1:11-13 (NIV)

Jesus sets a good example on how to serve people you have been called to but who do not recognize your assignment. He still gave what he had—salvation through repentance—on the off-chance that someone might recognize and accept that gift. Those who eventually come around are then conferred the status of sons and daughters of God. This new identity or birth is not as a result of human decision. This is our cue to serve our generation. Jesus Christ is our role model in reaching out and staying the course.

In answering the question of when to serve, we ought to discern the times and seasons we are in and take steps to serve, even when our target group do not hear us or see us. This is when we resolve ourselves to staying the course until we have run our race and finished the course.

If there was ever a time to serve our generation with what we have, it is now!

Chapter Eleven:
Harnessing Resources

One of the greatest deceptions we are fed centers on adequacy—the idea that we are unable to accomplish much (if not anything) in life, let alone the purpose or assignment we have been given to pursue. This is further exacerbated by a trend, which puts emphasis on how we look and feel about ourselves fueled mainly, in our time, by media.

Through the myriad ideals and perceptions thrown out there in these spheres, people are forced to really examine themselves to identify whether they have what it takes to live successful lives. This is when they are bombarded with ideals of what people should look like, what they should be able to accomplish in life (sometimes by a certain age), etc. These ideals are mostly promoted by people who claim to be the gatekeepers of modern living.

Unfortunately, in a world of fakery and pretense, which is what most of these influencers peddle around, we are often made to reexamine ourselves in the light of these ideals and how inadequate we are in ourselves and our ability to pursue anything worthwhile. This leads to all manner of self-inflicted problems such as lack of confidence, self-hatred, and the seeming idea that one cannot amount to anything when they compare themselves to these standards set by the gatekeepers. This is more prevalent among the emerging generation.

The truth of the matter is we all have immeasurable resources inside of us which can be deployed in accomplishing our goals which, among other things, includes serving our generation. And until we come to this realization, we will spend our entire life living out other people's lives or what they perceive to be their idea of life without realizing it. Therefore, we have a responsibility to ourselves to ensure that we get off that road other people have carved out for themselves and tell us is the right road to fulfilment. And in place, remind ourselves that the only source from where we can find proper validation of who we are and what we have been endowed with is the creator of our life, God.

Nobody else can do that for you!

One of the lessons you will learn from the Author of Life is that although we are created equal in his image and likeness, our journeys in life and the way we end up are not the same. In fact, it is highly possible to have siblings from the same mother and father who have different characteristics and temperaments. They also tend to have different abilities. You only need to have a look at the story of Jacob and Esau in the Book of Genesis to see this difference. While Esau grew up to become a skillful hunter, his brother Jacob *"was content to stay at home among the tents"* (Genesis 25:27, NIV). This is how God created us, and it is very important that we embrace our differences and consider them as strengths rather than weaknesses simply on the basis that one does not have the same abilities as someone else.

A better understanding of this basic truth will help us internalize our true worth and, more critically, how to reach into the deep recesses of our lives to draw these resources out. God is looking to us identifying these treasures and having done so, harnessing and deploying them in serving our generation effectively.

Throughout the Bible, there are many instances where men and women, aided by God, have been able to harness the resources they had and bring about change in the lives of people and the community as a whole. An example that readily comes to mind is Moses and his journey or redeeming of God's people from slavery in Egypt.

In the account in Exodus, Moses is chosen to be the instrument God uses to free the Israelites from four hundred years of bondage and servitude at the hands of the Egyptians, who were a powerful force at the time. Like most of us with our low sense of security and feelings of inadequacy, Moses was reluctant in accepting the mandate God had placed on him. On several occasions, he questioned whether

God had made the right decision in choosing him for a task which was clearly going to be difficult and challenging.

On two occasions, God instructed him to reach out for what he had, even if that was as simple as a shepherd's staff to demonstrate the power that had been given to him for the assignment. Exodus 4 verse 2 recounts:

> "Moses answered, 'What if they do not believe me or listen to me and say the LORD did not appear to you?' Then the LORD said to him, 'What is that in your hand'? 'A staff,' he replied. The LORD said, 'Throw it on the ground.'"

Exodus 4:1-3 (NIV)

God wanted to make sure that Moses knew the resources he had at his disposal to build a strong case for the mission. Among other things, which included God's presence and power, he also had the shepherd staff which became an instrument of demonstration of the power backing him. Pharaoh's heart may have been hardened; however, he recognized that this was a power not to be messed with. Indeed, it was through a series of these powerful demonstrations of God's power through the earthly vessel in Moses that finally broke his resolve and eventually led to the freeing of the Israelites from servitude.

We see another instance in which Moses is instructed to reach out for what is in his hand, a demonstration of God's power. At the edge of the Red Sea, which stood between the Israelites and the promised land of Canaan, and coming under intense pressure from the people because of what they said to Moses,

> "... 'was it because there were no graves in Egypt that you brought us into the desert to die? What have you done to us by bringing us out of Egypt? Didn't we say to you in Egypt, leave us alone; let us serve the Egyptians? It would have been better for us to serve the Egyptians than to die in the desert.'"

Exodus 14:11-12 (NIV)

And also from Egypt as Pharaoh led a contingent of soldiers and charioteers to recapture the Israelites and bring them back into slavery, God again reminded Moses to use the resource he had to bring redemption and victory for his people:

> "Then the LORD said to Moses, 'Why are you crying out to me? Tell the Israelites to move on. Raise your staff and stretch out your hand over the sea to divide the water so that the Israelites can go through the sea on dry ground.'"

Exodus 14:15-16 (NIV)

The resource here again was the humble shepherd staff which, simple as it was, became the instrument God used to create the path for the Israelites to go into freedom from slavery. This is what he wants us to realize. If all we have is a shepherd staff, that's what God wants us to deploy for the assignment on our lives.

Looking at the exchanges between God and Moses, it is very clear that he thought God was going to use something or someone special other than what he had in mind. In fact, we can say that Moses did not consider that the staff he had in his hand could be used as the solution to the situation they were in. Hence, the reason why God asked the question *"Why are you crying out to me?"* And more poignant was the follow-up instruction: *"Tell the Israelites to move on"* and then you use the staff to create the miracle passage for them to get through to the other side, which was the side of safety.

This provides a valuable lesson for us. To serve our generation and to do so effectively, we need to recognize the resources we have at our disposal—however small, insignificant, or mighty they might be for the mission. I am reminded of the lyrics to *"That's When,"* one of the songs of Alvin Slaughter, one of the pioneers of the modern gospel music genre, which summarizes the essence of harnessing what we have:

> *What's that you have in your hand?*
>
> *I can use it, if you are willing to lose it.*
>
> *Take the little that you have and make it grand.*
>
> *I am El-Shaddai and I'll more than supply your need*
>
> (Source: songlyrics.com)

So what do we have in our hands today? What do we have in our lives today? When we recognize it and unearth it, it may be as insignificant in our eyes as anything else we've ever had, God can multiply it a million times for us to use for the purpose for which he has given it to us to serve him by serving our generation.

Our Experiences of Life

You cannot serve someone with what you don't have. That much we know. However, what we often fail to realize is that the best treasure we have is the sum total of our lived experiences.

Thus, the experiences we have in our interaction with life serves as the best resource we have to draw upon when we are serving our generation. And if there was ever a time that the emerging generation needed shoulders to lean on into the future, it is now.

We are living in a time that presents us with enormous opportunities to do great things and the space for growth. This is largely informed by the huge strides or improvement in every facet of life—medicine, health, and technology, which has led to a boom in entrepreneurship as well as other technology-induced innovation just to mention a few. This has created enormous growth in imagineering and visioneering for those who are prepared to identify a gap in the market to use the business phrase, and come up with solutions to plug those gaps.

Unfortunately, this situation has also created a gap in the ability for people to figure out exactly what they want to be. There seems to be a lack of guidance, particularly among the emerging generation when it comes to the path or direction to take in their lives. For Christians, the question is always *"What is God's plan for my life?"*

While there may not be a one-size-fits-all answer to those questions, it is important that the experiences of people who have run the race before us be shared so that people can learn a thing or two about how they can also run their race. They may not be on the same path but learning from such experiences is invaluable as it equips them with a roadmap for their own journeys.

And this is where you come in...

Your life experience is one of the resources you have to serve your generation. What you have been through—the highs and the lows, the good, the bad and the ugly situations you have been in as well as the decisions you've had to make are a treasure throve which will come in handy for the emerging generation. With these experiences, it shows that the journey of life is not one filled with great experiences and memories but one which, when endured to the end, provides fulfilment, happiness, and joy to the person who has gone through it.

How can you encourage someone who is on the verge of losing their marriage if you have not been in that situation before and yet came out on the other side with such wisdom and dignity?

How can you inspire a young person who suffers from lack of confidence and self-esteem as they have never received any form of affirmation from home?

How do you mentor someone who has an idea to start a business but does not know where to begin if you don't have the experience yourself?

Or worse still, how do you deal with a business idea which started off very well and then folded up with all the debts and the personal problems associated with business failures if you haven't travelled on that road before?

As someone who has struggled with addiction (online pornography) and healed from it, I have learned a lot through the experience, particularly on the trigger points of addiction, the cycle of feeding the addiction, and the resultant feeling of guilt, self-rejection, and the feeling unworthy of love, particularly God's love. Over the last three and a half years, I've gradually crawled out of it, gaining the confidence and the power to break away from such destructive habits with the help of God, who gives me strength to fight and to keep persevering. I have also asked for accountability partners that I am answerable to who have come alongside me on the journey to recovery. I am and will ever be grateful to them for being part of the journey.

The experience has put me in a unique position to mentor and encourage young people who might be struggling with the same addiction—or any addiction for that matter. And if the current global pandemic and the associated lack of face-to-face community and social networks are anything to go by, there are a lot of people struggling with all forms of addictions out there and who need people who will help me on the journey to recovery and the rediscovery of themselves. They are crying out for mentors who will embrace them for who they are and not look at them with the eyes and mind of condemnation but rather with excitement. It is a great opportunity to serve them by helping them break out of the cycle of addiction.

They need someone who can understand where they are currently at to come alongside them, put their hand on their shoulder, and say to them "you will be alright! You are not on your own! I am here to help you on this journey." They don't need condemnation and judgment from people as they are already carrying the burden of shame and guilt. This is how we can become effective in serving our generation: offering our unique experiences at their disposal as a guide for their path.

Natural Law

The world is governed by natural law, and therefore, an understanding of these laws will help people succeed at what they set out to achieve. A failure to recognize these laws will invariably lead to a lot of pain, frustration, and heartache. One of such laws is the law of sowing and reaping.

Now, what I am about to say has nothing to do with the prosperity gospel, although there is a point in using this law to justify the theology or doctrine if you will. In the book of Genesis, God, the creator of the heavens and the earth (including humans) established a natural law that governs our lives today. With the destruction of the known world in the Great Flood, God initiates the beginning of human life again with its intrinsic natural law:

> *"As long as the earth endures, seed time and harvest, cold and heat, winter and summer, day and night will never cease."*
>
> Genesis 8:22 (NIV)

With this declaration, God set the stage for what would eventually become the way we live our lives and the fact that everything we do, or at least most of what we do, will hinge on this principle. The context might seem agricultural; however, its application transcends every facet of life.

In an agricultural sense, a farmer usually plants seeds. These then take root, spread, and produce fruits, usually after it has gone through seasons of germination, growth, and bearing of fruit. Once the fruit is harvested, the farmer does not eat everything because there won't be any to plant when the planting season comes around. So after the fruit is harvested, there is in the harvest the seed part and the food part. The seed part is kept and prepared for the next planting season while the food part is what the farmer enjoys with his family and might even sell some of it to earn money for the upkeep of his family. Should the farmer eat both the seed and the food parts of the harvest, he is likely to face problems as there won't be anything to plant or sow during the planting season. And there will also not be anything to be harvested since nothing was planted. This is what God instituted as natural law.

A young person who wants to make themselves competitive and attractive to prospective employers in the job market will have to apply this natural law of sowing and reaping. They need to sow their time, energy, and money to study a vocation, and this can be for a number of years. Five to seven years if you want to be a doctor, for example. They will need to build the resilience to stay the course without deviating. They might even take up a part-time job to raise some money for textbooks and also to pay their bills if they don't have a bank of mum and dad. This is the sowing part, which can sometimes be frustrating, hard work, and painful.

Then, at the end of the course, they graduate with good grades and then the dream job with the dream organization comes along as they come knocking on their door with all the perks—a good salary, a car, medical insurance, etc. This is the fruit or the harvest part of the law. What you will have will not be something thrown on your lap. Rather, it will be the result of the seed you sown into your education.

The same will go for entrepreneurship when you sow seeds of research and development at the initial stages of a business and what you have in the end is the harvest when you come up with a product or service which serves a need in the society.

Faith

Faith is the fuel you need to help in the journey of serving your generation. As Hebrews 11:6 rightly puts it:

> *"And without faith, it is impossible to please God because anyone who comes to him must believe that he exists and that He rewards those who earnestly seek him."*
>
> Hebrews 11:6 (NIV)

When we recognize that the assignment to serve our generation comes from him, we are empowered to move forward with our purpose. The rewards are the lives that are given a purpose because you manifested your purpose to serve. This is very important as the confidence to step out will rise and fall with your belief in the assignment you have been called to.

Messes as Messages

A person's mess can become the message needed to help bring direction and a sense of focus into someone's life. This falls within the remit of life experiences. When you learn about the mess of a person, however messy the situation may be, it often serves as a learning opportunity on how to avoid that situation. This could potentially be used as a treasure to serve one's generation. Do not despise or cover up the messes in your life. They can be used as a powerful message in how to live a purposeful life.

Throughout the journey in this book, the one fact that has been stressed quite a lot is the idea that we all have something on the inside of us which needs to be brought out as a vital resource to serve our generation effectively. We also have at our disposal our life experiences, our faith in God, natural law, and our mess, which constitutes the resources we can draw upon as we endeavor to serve our generation.

This, hopefully, will debunk the idea or feeling of inadequacy for the journey ahead. We've learned that it is not that we are inadequate; rather, we do not or have not realized that these seemingly mundane experiences can be very reliable resource for reaching our goal of mentoring the emerging generation for a life of significance and purpose.

Chapter Twelve: The Full Picture

In a sense, this is very important. At some point in a journey, one needs to stop, reset, recalibrate, release, and run (according to the author of Hebrews) with perseverance the race that is set before us. This is very important as it helps us to see the full picture or bigger picture of what we are about. We need to be reminded every so often so that we don't end up losing perspective and the momentum for the cause less we crash and burn.

The full picture. What this journey is about. What it means to serve our generation.

Throughout the course of this book, we have learned about how to live a life of purpose and significance by becoming selfless in serving our generation—a life lived on purpose and with significance.

In this book, we have looked at the various elements that goes into equipping people with power, knowledge, and resources to serve a generation or in some cases, generations yet unborn through actions taken today. Thus for us to fulfil our assignment in serving our generation effectively and efficiently, we must take note of the following:

Identify Who We Truly Are

You can only serve and do so effectively when you know who you are. This is very critical to the discourse as you cannot give what you don't have. A healthy dose of who you are empowers you with strength and perseverance to last long on the journey.

Make no mistake. This is a long journey, and you need to spend time knowing yourself, including your weaknesses and blind spots but also what resources you have to serve and leave a lasting legacy for posterity. And if you are not sure of all these things, then the best place to go to is the source of all things—God. If you lack the wisdom to help you get the full picture, then ask him (James 1:5). And when you ask him, he will surely answer you and show you great and mighty things you don't know (Jeremiah 33:3).

You also need to have a good dose of faith when you ask him for anything because you have to trust him wholeheartedly throughout the process. He only rewards those who believe he is capable of what you've asked him for and are diligent in their pursuit (Hebrews 11:6).

Identify Needs in the Community, Particularly Among the Emerging Generation

Jesus embodies what it means to identify the needs of a people and serve at that point of need. He set the standard for us to follow, the blueprint for us to use in our pursuit of the same. In Jesus, God saw the cry of the human soul after our identity was lost in the Garden of Eden. We lost what could have been the greatest partnership ever known between our creator and us. We are called by God to maintain and manage the earth for God. He made everything at our disposal. And yet, we fell short of his standards and so weren't able to hold the fort for him. From then on, things went from bad to worse and we were never the same again.

However, in his love and compassion, he kept the fire of the partnership burning in his heart. And having identified our hunger and desire to reconcile with him and thereby reignite the partnership, but falling short at each step, decided to send his son in human flesh to perform the ultimate sacrifice to achieve this goal. He did for our example.

Today, it behooves on us as passionate people to serve by first identifying the needs within our communities so that we can offer solutions to those problems and needs. This is by far the best we can live a life of purpose and a legacy for generations to come.

Look out for signs in the culture that show areas that need help.

Identify the People You Believe You Have Been Called To Serve

If you want to lose your point of effectiveness, then try to serve everybody you meet. You will burn out quickly and may end up becoming disillusioned. This is because you are not called to serve every generation. In other words, your assignment is not to all people.

David, the subject of our discussion, served his own generation by the will of God. The emphasis is on *own*. He served the people who were living in Israel during the time of his reign as king in Israel. This is what we need to understand. Otherwise, there will be people who may not identify with the assignment on your life. These are people who might end up frustrating or putting roadblocks in your way.

This is also the reason why you need to open your eyes and have a discerning spirit to identify the people you have been called to so that you will become effective in carrying out your God-ordained assignment. This cannot be stressed enough. It makes a huge difference between serving effectively and being frustrated, mediocre, and abandoning the mandate on your life.

Identify Where You Can Serve

Where you serve is equally as important as who you serve. You serve where your gifts are needed the most. You serve where the assignment on your life is valued and appreciated, even if that takes a while to resonate with your target audience. Perseverance is the key to enduring the journey and just serving your audience.

The community your target audience is, is where you serve. This among other things will include but not limited to the church, the community centers especially when we volunteer our time, skills, and talents in the service of the people.

The emerging generation are looking for authentic role models and mentors—people who are not afraid to acknowledge their flaws but also strive to live with integrity as enabled by God through the Holy Spirit. Your life becomes a walking and breathing testimony to the people you are leading and mentoring. This is very important.

Along the lines of mentorship is also sharing your experiences: the good, the bad, and the ugly with the emerging generation. Authenticity is being candid with the challenges, struggles, and failures you've dealt with and how that has propelled you into a greater influence for your generation. This strikes a chord with your target audience who might be in various stages in their life journey and who would do with such an example.

Identify When You Can Serve

There is never a specific time to serve our generation than a day called today and a time like now. Thus, we serve when the opportunity opens up for us to do so which is always now or today. If we fail to realize this, time will pass us by without us fulfilling the calling on our life.

To echo what King Solomon once said:

> *"Sow your seeds in the morning, and at evening, let your hands not be idle for you do not know which will succeed, whether this or that, or whether both will do equally well."*

Ecclesiastes 11:6 (NIV)

This Solomonic advice comes off the back of another one in which he reiterates the importance of serving now, not waiting until all is considered "perfect."

> *"Whoever watches the wind will not plant; whoever looks at the clouds will not reap. As you do not know the path of the wind or how a body is formed in a mother's womb, so you cannot understand the work of God, the maker of all things."*

Ecclesiastes 11:4-5 (NIV)

Serve your generation now, today, when you still have today, as there is never going to be a right time. Besides, tomorrow is never guaranteed to anyone!

So, the full picture is to identify the key elements of the journey and having done that, literally move ahead with steps to serve people in the here and now. Prayerfully consider these elements as you prepare for this incredible and life-fulfilling adventure

CALLED TO SERVE MY GENERATION

Chapter Thirteen:
Serving Our Generation in the Developing World

In a sense, this chapter puts flesh on all the principles and concepts shared in this book—the idea that a life of significance is usually a life of service and that we have a heavenly calling on our lives.

This chapter focuses on the practicalities of serving our generation and to a large extent, generations that are still to come. It focuses on where to find our assignment—who we have been called to serve in the practical sense of the word. Where better to serve than in an environment which will bring out the best and the worst in us in our quest to add value to people by serving them effectively and efficiently?

The emerging countries in the world offer a great opportunity for us to change our societies primarily through adding to people's lives. It is also the environment where problems and needs are identified and where, with the right environment, one can rise to the occasion in fulfilling their purpose, serving their generation in those environments. It is in those environments that their treasures will be recognized and appreciated.

In the Bible, there is a great example of someone who abandons his relative comfortable environment and opts to go to another environment with the purpose of serving generations in that environment. He does so by rallying the people to rebuild their identity and their sense of self-worth. This story is found in the book of Nehemiah in the Old Testament.

Nehemiah, a Hebrew, served as one of the trusted aides of the king of Persia. He is stirred by the problems in his ancestral homeland where the Jewish people had been pillaged so that their very identity as a nation and that of their territorial sovereignty was all but lost. These were represented by the walls of Jerusalem, walls that protected them as a people group with their unique culture and religion and which had been violently destroyed by their neighboring nations, leaving them on the brink of collapse.

Although Nehemiah was leaving a life of comfort in Persia, far removed from the situation happening back home, he still had a heart for his people. Why is that so?

A delegation from Jerusalem visited him to break the news of what had happened back home. This is how it is recorded in the Bible:

The words of Nehemiah son of Hakaliah:

In the month of Kislev in the twentieth year, while I was in the citadel of Susa, Hanani, one of my brothers, came from Judah with some other men, and I questioned them about the Jewish remnant that had survived the exile, and also about Jerusalem.

They said to me, "Those who survived the exile and are back in the province are in great trouble and disgrace. The wall of Jerusalem is broken down, and its gates have been burned with fire."

When I heard these things, I sat down and wept. For some days I mourned and fasted and prayed before the God of heaven. Then I said:

"Lord, the God of heaven, the great and awesome God, who keeps his covenant of love with those who love him and keep his commandments, let your ear be attentive and your eyes open to hear the prayer your servant is praying before you day and night for your servants, the people of Israel. I confess the sins we Israelites, including myself and my father's family, have committed against you. We have acted very wickedly toward you. We have not obeyed the commands, decrees and laws you gave your servant Moses.

"Remember the instruction you gave your servant Moses, saying, 'If you are unfaithful, I will scatter you among the nations, but if you return to me and obey my commands, then even if your exiled people are at

the farthest horizon, I will gather them from there and bring them to the place I have chosen as a dwelling for my Name.'

"They are your servants and your people, whom you redeemed by your great strength and your mighty hand. Lord, let your ear be attentive to the prayer of this your servant and to the prayer of your servants who delight in revering your name. Give your servant success today by granting him favor in the presence of this man."

I was cupbearer to the king.

Nehemiah 1:1-11 (NIV)

Nehemiah was stirred by the news he heard to serve his generation in his motherland. Such was the level of stirring that it led him to a time of mourning for his people, fasting and praying for divine guidance and direction, as he became restless about the situation and wanted to do something about it. At the same time, his faith made him recognize that he needed divine direction and guidance for what he was about to do.

Even more striking, he took it upon himself to become the intercessor for the Jewish people back in Jerusalem who, at this time, had lost all hope of any restoration and the reestablishment of their national identity as a people. Surely, if this is not a mark of someone who was clearly passionate and fired up about the state his people were in, I don't know what else it is. Nehemiah is clearly someone who never abandoned his roots even when he was living a high-profile life in a foreign land.

To cut a long story short, that prayer served as a catalyst for what would be an epic few months in which divine favor was powerfully at play when he won the approval of the king. The king made everything he needed for the massive project of rebuilding the walls of Jerusalem a possibility.

Simply put, the desire to serve his country men and women was so strong that he was ever so willing to abandon his high office to go to where he was clearly needed and where his resources would be acknowledged and celebrated. And this was confirmed when he found favor with his employer, King Artaxerxes, who provided all the resources, materials, and the infrastructure Nehemiah needed to help him embark on the project of reinstalling the identity and the territorial sovereignty of his people—the Israelites.

And though he faced strong opposition from every side, they were able to rebuild the walls in a record fifty-two weeks.

Why this story? Because it bears semblance to what is happening across nations in the developing world and, in particular, the continent of Africa. In a way, one can safely say that the walls of Africa are in ruin and in need of men and women whose hearts are stirred to build it so that it can once again regain its position as the cradle of human civilization.

The walls of Africa, through colonization (colonialism), internal conflicts and wars, poverty, deprivation, few resources, and poor leadership, lies in ruin. And like what happened in Jerusalem, the territorial sovereignty and its identity also lies in ruin from decades and centuries of exploitation. It is now in need of the Nehemiah of the continent, wherever they might be, whose hearts would be stirred to serving the continent by adding value to it and her people.

Like Nehemiah, will Africa appeal to her children across the seas to see and hear the desperate situation it is in? And would they heed the call to come and serve her emerging generation and the one yet to be born?

Strengths, Weaknesses, Opportunities, and Threats in Africa

The most naturally resourced and yet the most impoverished, Africa presents contrasting fortunes as it strives to reassert its position as the next giant gradually rising from the ashes. There are strengths, weaknesses, opportunities, as well as threats hanging over the continent, and this is more prevalent among the emerging generation. They are the one who would take on the mantle of their forebears to drive the agenda of the new continent forward – an agenda that will seek to shake off the often negative stereotype associated with the continent to one that offers great hope and opportunities for her youth who are her greatest asset.

Here are a few of the strengths, weaknesses, opportunities, and threats for the continent:
- Projections by the United Nations show that the world's population will hit 10 billion by 2055 [1]
- Approximately 95% of this growth will take place in low- and middle-income countries.
- Africa will account for 57% of the growth with an estimated growth of 1.4 billion (*could be all four!!*)
- In particular, the population of sub-Saharan Africa is projected to double by 2050—that constitutes around 99% increase.
- Almost 60% of Africa's population is under the age of *twenty-five*, making Africa the world's youngest continent.
- This growth is attributed to high fertility coupled with declining child mortality.
- The burgeoning youth population is both an opportunity and a challenge for the continent.
- A higher youth population is an opportunity for the continent to address Africa's sustainable development goals and challenges that come with such goals.
- While the continent's natural resources are vital, the creativity and innovation of its youthful population can play a key role in the continent's economic transformation.

These upbeat statistics are in sharp contrast to the reality on the ground. These might be both threats as well as opportunities for the continent:
- Sixteen million young Africans are facing unemployment.
- On average, an estimated 11 million young people join Africa's labor market each year, yet the continent generates only 3.7 million jobs annually. There is clearly a deficit.

---

[1] (Cities Alliance | Ending Urban Poverty and Promoting the Role of Cities, 2022).

- The informal sector provides for many African youth the only source of employment and means of earning a living. In sub-Saharan Africa, informal employment as a percentage of total employment is 89%.
- The hopelessness and frustrations of an unemployed young population can, in its extreme, have severe consequences not only in Africa but across the world. The recent migration of many African youths to Europe in search of greener pastures is a good example.
- The World Bank estimates that 40% of people who join rebel movements are motivated by lack of economic opportunities.
- The situation is also complex for young girls who may face a multitude of challenges including a lack of access to reproductive health services, education, and employment opportunities.
- The United Nations Development Programme (UNDP) estimates that $95 billion of revenue is lost annually due to gender inequalities in sub-Saharan Africa.
- There is an urgent need for the continent to prepare its young professionals for future roles as development leaders and change agents.
- The potential of the young population can only be harnessed if the continent creates conducive environments for the youth to take action.
- Youth employment, skills, and gender empowerment as priorities for national development. These key drivers are vital to the sustainability and development of the continent.

Clearly, there are incredible opportunities for the continent of Africa to readjust in order to rewrite the often-negative stereotypes associated with it. Make no mistake! Africa is going to be the continent of the not-too-distant future. It will be the continent with the youngest population on the planet. With such critical mass, it is gradually positioning itself for the next big thing. However, for this to really happen, there needs to be a massive drive aimed at preparing its greatest asset—her young, urban population as the success—or otherwise of the continent hinges heavily on a well-educated and savvy young population.

A critical area in the success of the continent is the creation of an enabling environment which appeals to the emerging generation. It is an environment which presents them with the opportunity to innovate and engineer for their peers and the continent as a whole. The emerging generation should be able to hear a message that says the continent is ready to pull all the stops to make them innovate and aspire to unearth their God-given abilities for the service of their fellow country men and women and ultimately for the continent.

Presently, there doesn't seem to be this environment created or being created on the continent. This situation is prompting the emerging generation to flee the continent in search of this enabling environment in industrialized countries in Europe and North America. This leaves the continent deprived of her children, the ones on whose shoulders the responsibility of building a better Africa rests on. This is often at the cost of their lives.

And the many that make it to the Promised Land, hope is immediately replaced by frustration at the lack of opportunities often limiting them to the bare minimum. Many have wondered if the life portrayed in the west primarily seen through the eyes of Hollywood and the western media is all that it's cracked up to be as they see a different western culture to the ones they were fed with.

Make no mistake! There are efforts by governments across the continent to try to plug the gap and make the country and the continent attractive once again to her children. But there is also a sense in which the youth of Africa feel their leaders are not doing enough and not quick enough to change their fortunes right across the continent. Some have taken to different platforms aided by technology to vent their frustration at the slow pace of change or the lack of it.

From demonstrations in Eswatini (formerly the Kingdom of Swaziland) in July 2021 for a change in leadership from an absolute monarchy to a full-fledged constitutional democracy to the *#EndSARS* protests and demonstrations in Nigeria and #FixTheCountry protest in Ghana, there seems to be a disconnect between leadership on the continent and the emerging generation for whom leadership was elected to serve. This leads to the breeding of discontent for African leaders.

The youth in Africa need to be inspired to dream again. They need to feel that there is hope for their future and that with the right attitude and mindset, coupled with hard work, they can thrive on the continent without leaving the shores of Africa for greener pastures elsewhere.

The youth in Africa are crying out for a Nehemiah out there who would come in and inspire them to rebuild their walls whiles at the same time building the walls of their countries and the continent as a whole. They need motivators and doers who inspire them on their journey of self-discovery and purpose. It is when they are able to discover who they are and what they carry on the inside that they will be equipped with the resources to open the door for the next generation to travel that path.

The youth in Africa need inspiration on so many levels!

Leadership

Both personal and corporate leadership are vital cogs in the wheel of development across the continent, and although a lot has been done to address the issue, there is still a lot more ground to cover. Far too often, we see and hear about leadership, especially at the corporate and governmental levels being misused. Often times, these abuses lead to an overall sense of underdevelopment and lack of opportunities for those for whom the government was elected to serve in the first place. This is a common scene across the continent.

The youth are watching with anger and frustration as, increasingly, African leaders sacrifice vital national development programs and youth empowerment policies on the altar of selfish ambition, mismanagement of the resources of the continent, as well as a willful disregard for the people at the heart of a leader's focus.

They want new leadership on the continent, the type of leadership where the development of a nation as well as the creation of an enabling environment conducive for creativity, innovation, and the needed support is given the utmost priority. These are some of the recipe for youth engagement, which leads to the development of a country and the continent as a whole.

Education

An educated youth is the biggest asset for a country, and this is so crucial for Africa since it is the continent with the youngest population, with the trend set to continue into the next few decades. The youth need to be upskilled to take advantage of the coming wealth transfer which is beginning to take place on the continent.

And by education, what is required is a set of curricula, which will prioritize the leading issues besetting the continent with the aim of training the youth to offer viable solutions to them. Thus, African education to solve Africa's problems should be at the heart of this.

When presented well, it will attract the emerging generation to take up the mantle and be the solution carriers for the continent.

Mentors and Role Models

Nothing inspires as much as seeing someone like you, mostly from a similar background serving their generation and making an impact on people around the world, people who are changing society one way or another and who are influencing people by adding value to them. Sadly, though, there aren't enough of these trend-setters on the continent, and neither do we have enough around the world.

In business and entrepreneurship, for instance, the emerging generation needs to see a lot of people of African descent making a real difference in their sphere of endeavors in business and entrepreneurship on the continent and around the world. They are more likely to be inspired on their own business and entrepreneurial journey. The African youth need to see people from the continent as well as people of African descent make it to *Oxbridge* (a coinage for those who go to Oxford or Cambridge Universities in the United Kingdom) and who have gone ahead to set up businesses and enterprises and are making waves in the world.

And this is where the *diaspora* come in.

The Diaspora—Africa's Nehemiah?

In line with one of the fundamental questions asked on the journey to serve our generation, there is a huge role the diaspora can play in serving their generation on the continent by helping to push the continental development agenda forward.

Nehemiah abandoned his relatively privileged life and went to where his skills, resources, and passion were needed. As a result, he was able to rally his people to rebuild the walls of Jerusalem under intense intimidation and pressure from those who were bitterly opposed to the project.

But who are the diaspora, you may ask?

Simply put, a diaspora is a large group of people with a similar heritage or homeland who have since moved out to places all over the world. In other words, they are people who share the same heritage in terms of where they come from, and this can be both nationality and continent wise, who move away from their original geographical area for various reasons and in some way or form still maintain links to their motherland.

The term "diaspora" comes from an ancient Greek word meaning "to scatter about." And that's exactly what the people of a diaspora do—they scatter from their homeland to places across the globe, spreading their culture as they go. The Bible refers to the diaspora of Jews exiled from Israel by the Babylonians. In modern era, the word is used more generally to describe any large migration of refugees, language or culture.

On July 5, 1950, the Israeli government passed a law which became known as the *Law of Return*. The law gave Jews around the world the right to relocate to Israel, the Motherland, and acquire citizenship. Section 1 of the Law of Return declared that "every Jew has the right to come to this country (Israel) as an *Oleh (immigrant)*". The law enabled millions of Jews around the world to return to their homeland

and with it, the critical mass of skills, experience, and wealth to help develop the nation into what it is today.

There is a strong case for a similar "Right of Return" for Africa's diaspora.

Indeed, currently, there is a large African diaspora around the world whose expertise is needed on the continent to help in its development agenda.

There are primarily two categories of the African diaspora—the ones who were born and raised on the continent and for various reasons including economic advancement, later migrated to the west, mainly to Europe and North America, but increasingly to Asia. The other category is mainly the descendants of those who were at the receiving end of the trans-Atlantic slave trade that took place in the early fifteenth century through to the nineteenth century. Many of them settled in America, the Caribbean Islands, South America, and in Europe. Many people from this category are now tracing their ancestry back to the continent, actively engaging with their brothers and sisters on the ground, and contributing productively towards the development of Africa.

This is a ground swell of resource that Africa has and which it needs at this pivotal time in its history.

There are similarities between what Nehemiah did and what the African diaspora can do to help rebuild the broken walls of Africa. The need for collaboration between the diaspora and those on the continent is far greater today than it has ever been in centuries.

However, for this to take off, there needs to be genuine desire and passion for the project. Like Nehemiah, the called out diaspora's need to prayerfully consider what is at stake before they put their hands to the plough. This is because one needs to develop the resilience and mental toughness needed to start, but more importantly, to see the rebuilding through to the end.

How can you answer the call? Where can you answer the call to rebuild the walls of Africa? With what (resources and skills) can you do that?

To answer these questions, it is important to realize that you have been brought to this hour in Africa's history for a purpose. So that if you are a student learning a skill, know that the knowledge and skills you are acquiring is not only for you to find a job and live your life, although these are very important too. There is a far greater purpose for that knowledge or that skill. It is for you to serve your generation on the continent so that by adding value to their lives, they are also empowered to do the same creating a ripple effect in the process.

If you are an aspiring writer with a burning purpose of serving your generation with the concept, ideas, and content you produce, you have to consciously create content that inspires the generation you are targeting to rise up and start taking action, embarking on their journey of discovery and adding value to humanity. A person should read your book and find enough instructions on how to navigate their way through life but also enough inspiration to start the process of self-discovery and working to help others do the same. So that when you finally see corruption as David did (Acts 13:36), your legacy will stand the test of time and people will say of you that you served your generation by the will of God.

As you read this book, I do hope you have found it enriching and encouraging, that it has inspired you to make the necessary changes in your life so that you can inspire yourself as well others around you to also serve their generation.

Go and serve your generation by the will of God and with the treasures you have on the inside of you. Leave a legacy for posterity. Enrich the world by the people you impact with the treasure you have in you and see *corruption* with fulfilment and dignity

ABOUT AUTHOR

Emmanuel Donkor is an Author, Speaker, Trainer and Youth Leader who is passionate about calling out the emerging generation to deploy their potential for a more fulfilling life. He believes that a life lived with purpose is usually one that is lived when we add value to others by serving them.

He believes that a life that is well lived is when one devotes themselves to adding value to other people and this is done by serving. Thus, a life of purpose is one lived when we are of service to others. When we start to serve one another that is when a higher call to purpose is placed on us. This is why he has devoted his life to serving his generation and the next one by adding value to them through offering his expertise, experiences as well as mentoring.

Also known as 'Manny', Emmanuel has a bachelor's degree in English and Theatre Arts from the University of Ghana and a Master's degree in Communications from Westminster University in London. In addition to these, he also has a certificate in Christian Entrepreneurship from the Joseph Business School, London at the Dominion Centre in Wood Green, North London where he was adjudged the best student at the class of 2014.

Manny also has a certificate of English Language Teaching to Adults (CELTA) awarded by Cambridge University where he currently lives. This has enabled him to teach English as a foreign language (EFL) to many learners from all over the world for over 7 years mainly in London and Cambridge as his passion is teaching, training and learning and development. He is currently a student member of the Chartered Institute of Personnel and Development (CIPD) UK with a special interest in Learning and Development (L&D). He hopes to use the skills and training from CIPD to help equip businesses and organizations skill up their workforce in the Knowledge Economy.

As a day job, he is a corporate trainer at Cambridge University Hospital Hospitals NHS Foundation Trust where he is part of a team that trains clinicians (doctors, nurses and other allied health professionals) on their use of Epic which is the electronic patient record system as part of the digitalization of patient care in the UK

www.ingramcontent.com/pod-product-compliance
Lightning Source LLC
Chambersburg PA
CBHW031422290426
44110CB00011B/483